BOARD LIABILITY

Guide for Nonprofit Directors

Daniel L. Kurtz

Moyer Bell Limited
Mt. Kisco, New York

Published by Moyer Bell Limited.

First Edition

Library of Congress Cataloging-in-Publication Data

Kurtz, Daniel L.
    Board liability : guide for nonprofit directors /
    Daniel L. Kurtz.
    Includes index.
    1. Directors of corporations—Legal status, laws,
etc.—United States. 2. Corporations, Nonprofit—United
States. 3. Liability (Law)—United States. I. Title.
KF1388.7.Z9K87 1988   346.73'064—dc19   [347.30664]   87-35022

ISBN 0-918825-65-2 cl
0-918825-66-0 pb

Printed in the United States of America

Grateful appreciation to the following foundations and
corporations who helped support this book: Carnegie
Corporation of New York (which does not take
responsibility for any statements or views expressed in the
book), Robert Sterling Clark Foundation, Equitable
Financial Companies, The Ford Foundation, The New
York Community Trust, and The New York Times
Company Foundation.

CONTENTS

FOREWORD

In 1984, the members of the Committee on Non-Profit Organizations of the Association of the Bar of the City of New York recognized the need for a handbook discussing the rationale for, and statutory underpinnings of the potential liabilities of directors and officers of nonprofit organizations. Many individuals asked to serve as directors and officers of such organizations had misconceptions regarding their potential liability, and these hampered their assessment of the need for indemnification provisions in the organization's bylaws and directors' and officers' liability insurance. Given the importance of these issues to the nonprofit sector, the committee decided to sponsor an independent examination of the legal considerations involved in directors' and officers' liability.

The committee consulted with Daniel L. Kurtz, a former Assistant Attorney General for the Charities Bureau of the State of New York and a frequent lecturer and writer on the subject of directors' and officers' liability. Mr. Kurtz agreed to undertake an in-depth study of the problem and to prepare a report of his findings. Funding for this project was obtained through generous grants from the Carnegie Corporation of New York, the Robert Sterling Clark Foundation, the Equitable Financial Companies, The Ford Foundation, The New York Community Trust, and The New York Times Company Foundation. The committee takes this opportunity to express its deep appreciation for this support.

FOREWORD

The handbook is the result of this undertaking. The committee believes that this handbook will be of use to lawyers and others faced with legal questions involving the potential liability of directors and officers and nonprofit organizations. The committee also believes that this report will be a useful tool for legislators and other policy makers in considering legislation affecting this important area.

Committee on Non-Profit Organizations
Association of the Bar of the
  City of New York
Carolyn C. Clark, Chair
Peter deL. Swords, Former Chair
Vivian L. Cavalieri, Secretary

PREFACE

This book is a guide to the legal principles that govern the liabilities of directors and officers of charitable organizations and has been written primarily for those innumerable volunteers who are recruited each year for leadership positions in nonprofit organizations.

Several factors have created an urgent need for a book that offers guidance for those in nonprofit organizations and practical information on their board responsibilities and possible liabilities. These factors include the explosive growth in nonprofit organizations, particularly those involved with entrepreneurial activities, renewed emphasis by government on private and voluntary action, and an unprecedented insurance crisis leading to new areas of liability for individual directors.

This book is written for the broad middle range of the philanthropic world: institutions involved in health care, education, the arts, public policy issues and the like. Without attempting to deal with the needs of the largest institutions with ample resources and access to sophisticated counsel and small organizations with virtually no staff and, often, only fleeting existence, there remain tens of thousands of others with ambitious programs and modest resources for which counsel and guidance are lacking or available sporadically, and, then, only at substantial cost to other efforts. This book is intended to respond to the needs of this audience. It seeks to explain for nonlawyers the legal doctrines that bear on the responsibilities and liabilities of directors—what they mean, how they work, and the likely consequences of violating them—and it offers suggestions for avoiding liability.

While the definition of what is charitable may be a bit fuzzy around the edges, there is broad agreement on what is considered to be the core of this group: the schools, hospitals, religious institutions, cultural organizations, social services agencies, and advocacy and public policy groups that are commonly known as "501(c)(3) organizations" (the reference indicates the principal Internal Revenue Code section defining charitable organizations). Although there are many other varieties of "nonbusiness," "nonprofit," and "exempt" organizations to which portions of this book may apply (for example, social clubs, fraternal organizations, trade associations, labor unions, even governments themselves), it was written for charities specifically. To avoid definitional wrangling, I have chosen to call the organizations about which I am writing "nonprofits."

Much of this book describes the "duties" of directors, the violation of which may lead to the imposition on directors of liabilities, and examples that illustrate in a realistic way how such liabilities arise and may be avoided. It is impossible to do justice to the complexity of this subject simply by laying out some basic precepts. Being a good director is not a matter of adhering to a few unequivocal rules of conduct (go to meetings, dissent on the record, etc.). It is a dynamic responsibility that exists in a context that itself is constantly changing. What I have done is to describe, by exposition and example, the broad guiding legal principles and how the process of directing should work.

The prevailing model of corporate governance is not the charitable organization, but the business corporation. Because there is relatively little law pertaining specifically to nonprofits to guide us, we must look inevitably to corporate law as it pertains to business organizations, modified to reflect the distinctive legal characteristics of both nonprofits and their directors.

To convey a complete picture of the nature of directors' duties, the guide begins with brief chapters that provide an overview of the nonprofit sector, identifying the characteristics that distinguish nonprofits, discussing how boards are organized and composed, and describing the functions that nonprofit boards perform. It then explains under what circumstances directors can be sued and, finally, what can be done to protect them when they are sued. The case studies in chapter 4 help to illustrate the legal principles discussed, especially those in chapters 4, 5 and 6.

This guide discusses the responsibilities and liabilities both of directors of charitable organizations and their officers—often, but not always, the same persons. In general, the standards of conduct expected of officers and directors, as well as the potential liabilities they face, are the same, although the functions they perform may be quite different. For purposes of convenience, therefore, rather than referring innumerable times to "directors and officers," we will refer only to "directors" when we mean "officers and directors," unless the context clearly dictates otherwise. The term directors is intended to refer to all individuals serving on a nonprofit organization's governing board, whether they are called directors, trustees, governors, regents, or whatever.

Although this volume is not intended primarily for lawyers, it should be useful for those who do not deal regularly with nonprofits and their legal needs. Extensive, often textual, notes at the end of the book add a dimension to this volume that should be of interest even to expert practitioners in the area.

ACKNOWLEDGEMENTS

Only now have I come to understand fully and appreciate the extent to which a book like this truly is the product not just of its author, but of a collaborative effort. The collaborators range from those who contributed early inspiration and ideas to those who assisted in the production process and include many others along the way.

Of all those formally connected to this project, I first would like to acknowledge the role of the Committee on Non-Profit Organizations of the Association of the Bar of the City of New York, under whose auspices I wrote this book. In particular, I'd like to thank its immediate past and current Chairs, Peter deL. Swords and Carolyn C. Clark. Peter was a major conceptual influence on the project and Carolyn ably saw this volume through to completion. While many of the more than fifty committee members who served from 1984 to 1987 were supportive, I owe special thanks to the Publication Subcommittee, which met with me regularly over the life of this project: Antonia Grumbach, George Kaufman, Max Kempner and Jane Gregory Rubin. Of equal importance were the foundations and corporations that generously supported the project. Without their contributions this book would not exist.

On the production end, I'd like to thank especially Nancy Laube, who repeatedly word-processed my near-illegible jottings into a clear manuscript, my editor, Chauncey G. Olinger, Jr., who made

ACKNOWLEDGEMENTS

me explain myself, and my publisher, Jennifer Moyer, whose varied talents, from editing to marketing, made this book.

Then, there are those who, although not formally involved in this effort, performed invaluable service: my student assistant/ researcher, Kannan Menon, for his indefatigable (and tedious) labor; Professor Harvey Goldschmid, of the Columbia University School of Law, for his special insight into issues of governance; Barbara Scott Preiskel for patiently recounting her experiences as a director; David Kellogg of the Council on Foreign Relations, who educated me about publishing; my partners at Lankenau Kovner & Bickford who patiently forbore from making reasonable demands on my time so I could complete this project; my friend, Professor Lawrence M. Grosberg of the New York Law School, who gave me sanctuary to rewrite the manuscript away from all distractions; and my wife, Elizabeth Olofson, whose better judgment often prevailed at critical junctures and who also graciously bore the extra burdens of family life.

None of those whose support and assistance contributed to making this book possible bears any responsibility for any statement made or views expressed here; they are solely the author's.

Chapter 1

AN OVERVIEW
OF THE NONPROFIT SECTOR

The Range of the Nonprofit World

There exists no wholly reliable census of the number of non-profit organizations nationally. The Internal Revenue Service, the most comprehensive collector of data in this field, treats as nonprofit more than two dozen distinct varieties, a total of almost 800,000. And this figure excludes most churches and many other religious organizations, the addition of which would increase these numbers by almost 50 percent.[1]

Even within the 300,000 or so charitable nonprofits, there is an almost bewildering variety of types and sizes. On the one hand, there are the major exemplars of America's high civilization: the grant-making foundations with vast endowments, our preeminent educational institutions, the largest, most complex, and sophisticated centers for medical care and research, the leading institutions of both established culture and experimentation in the arts. On the other hand, there are the myriad community-based organizations, grass-roots providers of social services, day care, housing for the poor, job training.

Charity is practiced in the religious activities of millions of Americans on a daily basis; it channels enormous sums of money into research on, and the treatment of, every conceivable psychological and somatic ailment. And there is that uniquely American phenomenon—what we now call advocacy organizations—first identified by de Tocqueville in his observation on our propensity to associate for the promotion of a cause. Whether it has been temperance, nuclear

1

disarmament, opposition to slavery, or the right to work, advocacy organizations have been and continue to be at the forefront of virtually every public issue.

From an economic perspective, nonprofits produce a dazzling array of goods and services. Although still largely unmeasured, their contribution is substantial; total nonprofit revenues may well approach $200 billion nationally, and total nonprofit assets are substantially higher.[2] Nonprofits dominate certain occupational and geographic markets. In particular fields, nonprofit organizations are major employers—for example, almost 15 percent of professional and technical employees work for nonprofits and in particular industries— educational services for example—nonprofits account for as much as 90 percent of all jobs.[3]

In recent years, a number of theories have been proffered by legal scholars, philosophers, economists, sociologists, and others to account for and to explain nonprofits. Some see them as filling interstices in the free market economy, while others see nonprofits as functioning essentially outside the free enterprise system.[4] Fortunately, for our purposes, it is not necessary to resolve this increasingly complex debate. As stated by Lord McNaghten in the nineteenth century:

> "Charity" in its legal sense comprises four principal divisions: trusts for the relief of poverty; trusts for the advancement of education; trusts for the advancement of religion; and trusts for other purposes beneficial to the community not falling under any of the preceding heads.[5]

The fourth of these common law categories—of public benefit—is universally recognized as the key to defining charitable activity and "may be applied to almost anything that tends to promote the well-doing and well-being of social man."[6]

The Essential Characteristics of Nonprofits

Almost all charitable organizations are created under the separate legal systems of the fifty states and the District of Columbia.

While there are differences from state to state, most state laws provide for: (1) the limitation of activities to the pursuit of specified objectives benefiting the public (the "mission"), and (2) the prohibition on the distribution by nonprofits of any earnings or profits for private purposes (the "nondistribution constraint").

Some states permit the incorporation of charitable organizations with a charter proclaiming only a simple general statement of purpose; others require greater specificity. However, even those organizations formed with only a "general purpose" clause will have to submit a detailed description of proposed activities when seeking tax exemption from the Internal Revenue Service.[7] Virtually all state laws and the Internal Revenue Code impose some variation of the nondistribution constraint on nonprofit activities.

The "mission" and the "nondistribution constraint" largely define the character of nonprofit organizations. The importance of the relationship between organizational objectives and board conduct can be seen most clearly by a comparative examination of the nonprofit organization with the business corporation.

Profit-Making and Nonprofit Corporations

As described in a recently completed landmark study of corporate governance, the "business corporation is an instrument through which capital is assembled for the activities of producing and distributing goods and services and making investments . . . with a view to enhancing corporate profit and shareholder gain."[8] This prescription marks them off from nonprofit corporations, where there are a multiplicity of specific missions. Shareholders, by and large, do not care whether the objectives of a business enterprise are met by making widgets or wickets, cars or cucumbers.

The current trend in corporate nomenclature emphatically underscores this point. Today, for example, American Tobacco is American Brands, International Harvester is Navistar, and U.S. Steel is USX. The kind of business actually pursued is almost irrelevant. The corporation simply becomes a means to attain superior financial results, not an industry specific end. For nonprofits, while there is legitimate and increasing concern with financial performance, the pursuit of particular objectives—the "mission"—remains paramount, even when it is not legally binding.[9]

The ability to ascertain progress toward attaining objectives also is a critical difference between business and nonprofit organizations. Business activities are uniformly translated into a "bottom line." For nonprofits, there are no adequate measurements of the key nonfinancial objectives.[10] No one measurement of performance or even series of measurements can tell a university how well it is doing its job, or an environmental organization what its influence is on the quality of the environment much less on public discourse. Consequently, whether directors are doing their jobs capably is not always easy to judge.

The pursuit of profit-maximizing behavior by business organizations is an obligation due only to the corporation's shareholders. Shareholders may subordinate this pursuit to allow for social objectives (like corporate philanthropy).[11] However, unlike business organizations, which are owned by their shareholders collectively, *no* individual has a proprietary interest in nonprofits.[12] The general public is the ultimate beneficiary of the activities of charitable organizations. It is the public—that broad yet undefined class—that benefits from the goods and services that nonprofits provide. When fundamental nonprofit objectives are altered, the participation and assent of some representative of the general public—for example, a state attorney general—and the agreement of a court may be required.

The use of the corporate form by charities has many advantages.[13] Apart from tax-based considerations, incorporation solves many of the same problems that it does for private entrepreneurs: limited liability, organizational continuity, administrative convenience, familiarity, etc. However, there are fundamental differences in the two distinct types of endeavors. The business corporation remains our dominant form of economic organization and the preferred instrument for capital formation; nonprofit corporations, while also needing capital to sustain their activities, pursue a multitude of goals.[14]

4

Chapter 2

THE COMPOSITION AND STRUCTURE OF NONPROFIT BOARDS

The characteristics of those who serve on nonprofit boards (their composition) and the organization of boards into committees (their structure) are important factors in understanding director responsibility and liability. Nonprofit board structure, designed to facilitate both performance of board functions and compliance by directors with their duties, reflects what is unique about the composition of nonprofit boards. These distinctive attributes become important determinants of director liability because the relevant standards of conduct for directors apply flexibly to each individual director's particular circumstances (see chapter 4).

Board Service and Composition

The boards of directors of nonprofit corporations seem similar to their business counterparts, but there are striking differences. Role, size, term and security of office, and compensation all have important consequences for nonprofit governance and director liability.

The law generally places no limits on the size of a corporate board, although in many states there is a minimum number of directors required.[1] Nonprofit boards, with some categorical exceptions (for example, private foundations), however, tend to have substantially larger boards than business corporations which have an average of thirteen.[2] One such survey puts the average size of nonprofit boards at upwards of thirty; another fixes it at slightly more than thirty-four.[3] Exceptions are the small and medium-sized foundations, particularly those with strong ties to their creators or the creators' families with only a handful of members.

The American free enterprise system maintains at least a semblance of shareholder democracy with the proxy fight a potent, if sporadically employed, tool to assure the accountability of corporate management.[4] In contrast, most nonprofits have no members and the directors commonly choose their own successors.[5] Assuming no serious misconduct on their part or other misfortune sufficiently egregious to call public attention to their service, directors often have life tenure. Some organizations, however, have express policies in their by-laws limiting the number of terms or years of service of directors.

Service for directors of nonprofit organizations is typically uncompensated, again with the exception of directors serving on private foundation boards.[6] By contrast, a 1985 survey reported average annual compensation for business directors of about $19,000. Only 12 percent of the business directors surveyed received less than $11,000 annually and 20 percent were paid more than $25,000.[7]

Another distinctive feature of nonprofit board service is their "independence": directors are not generally employees subject to the will of the organization's chairman nor do they have significant business or financial relationships with the organization. With, perhaps, the sole exception of a staff director, board members generally are "outsiders" (not employees of the organization). By contrast, the boards of directors of most large business corporations, while now possessing a majority of outside directors, still have significant representation from within the corporation, generally from the ranks of senior officers.[8]

The conventional wisdom for nonprofit organizations is that board members should not be employees of the organization.[9] The virtual absence of "insiders" on the typical nonprofit board carries with it the same consequences it does for business corporations: it impedes the direct flow of information from working officers and staff to board members.[10] When coupled with a small staff, typical of many nonprofit groups, the nonprofit board member may have but a single source—the chief staff officer—for information concerning the fiscal and programmatic health of the organization.

The effectiveness of a board in carrying out its responsibilities depends upon its capacity to evaluate objectively organizational accomplishments and management and staff performance. Because this is much more difficult to do when there is no arm's-length relationship between board members and the organization, or the board and its full-time employees, the typical nonprofit board structure avoids this problem.[11]

The Need for Committees

Board size, noncompensation, the lack of electoral accountability, and the numerical dominance of outsiders should be taken into account when considering the optimal nonprofit board structure.[12] A board is most effective when it is limited in size and composed predominantly of independent outside directors who make full use of staffed committees and outside experts.

While nonprofit board size is not limited by law, most state laws appear to encourage a collegial decision-making process by the board: proxy voting by directors is typically forbidden;[13] a minimum numerical membership for both boards and committees is the general rule, ensuring at least the semblance of a consultative process;[14] minimum quorum requirements for the conduct of board or committee business enhance the likelihood of representative action; and telephone conferences in lieu of actual meetings require all participants be able to hear each other.[15]

Experience has shown that the nonprofit board of thirty-plus members is too unwieldy to exercise its responsibilities effectively; it does not permit any meaningful exchange of views or, given the usual lack of staff assistance, the timely dissemination of useful information. Overly large boards encourage a nonquestioning, uninvolved role for most directors.

What is likely to happen in such a situation is that the real burdens of the board fall on a small number of directors and staff (including the staff head). Even well-intentioned directors may feel overburdened and become inattentive. The swollen nonprofit board simply encourages too great a diffusion of responsibility in which individual duty is just not keenly felt.[16]

The experience of publicly-held business corporations bears this out. The inactivity of the typical corporate director of twenty years past is a fading memory.[17] Many corporate boards are anything but rubber stamps and corporate service demands increasing time and attention.[18] This fact is reflected in the increased level of reported attendance by directors in fulfilling their duties as corporate directors. These directors possess, if not perfect attendance records, creditable ones, which manifest a clear commitment to their corporate responsibility.[19] While some of the diligence of corporate boards may be attributable to the fees their directors receive, most typically do not need the lure of the additional modest compensation.[20] By contrast, high levels of attendance at nonprofit board meetings is an unfamiliar phenomenon.

The size of the typical nonprofit board and its other distinctive aspects—uncompensated service, the independence of members, the self-perpetuating method of election—justify the extensive use of committees to do a substantial proportion of their real work. A well-organized committee structure is the key to effective performance.[21] The use of committees allows for a more intense and sustained scrutiny of particular issues, and better utilization of specialized knowledge possessed by individual directors.[22] The use of committees also facilitates the flow of information to the full board. Nonprofit laws provide ample authority for the prevalence of this structure.

Directors Are Monitors, not Managers

Because directors do not actually manage organizations, nonprofit statutes confer on boards of directors the authority to create committees and appoint officers and to assign to both a broad range of duties and functions. Recent nonprofit statutes, like California's and the Revised Model Nonprofit Corporation Act (RMNCA), recite explicitly that corporate affairs are managed under board authority.[23] Even in those states with a more archaic model of governance, it is unlikely that the law would require directors actually to manage an organization, as opposed to superintending its management by others.

In addition to this authority to delegate, boards often rely on outside experts, like lawyers, accountants and engineers, to develop and evaluate information as the basis for board (or committee) decision-making.[24] The delegation to others by directors of decision-making responsibilities as well as the reliance by directors on others for information and advice occurs in a wide variety of situations. In performing their functions, directors must rely on information, reports and statements from other persons (an outside accountant evaluating financial matters, for example) and from committees of the board (for example, the audit committee to evaluate the performance of the organization's auditors). Directors not serving on a particular committee have to rely on that committee's work—for example, the audit committee would have to assess if any serious financial problems surfaced in the management review performed annually by the auditors.

At the same time, noncommittee members must be concerned with the committee's specific decisions and judgments. For example, are the auditors' fees out of line? Even in constructing the agenda for its own deliberations—what matters it should address and how such items should be selected for board consideration—directors must rely on the decisions, judgments, or performance of other persons. While directors may be able to add items to an agenda at the start of a meeting, typically it has been constructed primarily by the chief staff officer in consultation with the board chair.

Although a decision to delegate responsibility to committees and others is usually embodied in a written board resolution, formal procedures need not be required.[25] A board may want to establish formal written criteria for identifying an item for the agenda, such as either a major action for board authorization (for example, capital construction program) or an oversight concern to be looked into (for example, the loss of a major funding contract). Or the board may simply instruct a senior staff member to report to it any major trouble spots relating to that staff member's area of responsibility. Both are equally valid ways of operating.*

---

*Reliance and delegation, as they relate to the duty of care, are discussed in detail in case studies A, B and C in chapter 4.

Basic Oversight Committees

Although state laws permit great flexibility in the creation of committees, they do not require their use.[26] With certain statutory exceptions, however, committees may possess all the power and authority of the full board, subject to any limitations made by board resolution or by limiting language in the by-laws. Thus, an executive committee may do almost anything a full board can. For those nonprofit boards, which, by virtue of their size and broad geographic dispersion, may have trouble assembling on short notice to deal with critical issues, the power of committees to take such action is especially important.

The basic committees most large boards should have are an executive committee and two oversight committees, audit and nominating.[27] Many boards also have fundraising and development committees (if dependent on public support), investment committees (if endowed), personnel or employee benefit committees, and one or more program committees (a museum for example, might have a collections committee; a university, an academic affairs committee; a public-interest legal organization, a litigation committee).

The executive committee usually is granted the right to perform all of the management responsibilities of the full board at those times when the board cannot function, or if it is too unwieldy to function on a regular basis. The number of executive committee members needed for a quorum and the place of such meetings should be set so that the committee's members are accessible and available with relative ease. For example, a national organization should not create an executive committee whose members, by virtue of where they live, are unable to assemble on short notice. Nevertheless, because it has the broadest authority of all committees, it should be as representative as possible of the full board.

Two committees in particular exercise critical oversight responsibilities: the audit committee and the nominating committees. Because an audit committee is chiefly responsible for maintaining an organization's financial integrity, its members should be independent (that is, neither employees of the organization nor those with substantial business relationships to it). While the chief staff officer and chief financial officer (if there is one) may attend audit committee meetings, they should not be committee members. Likewise, the nominating committee should have only independent members because of its role in selecting board candidates and the chief staff officer.

The audit committee is principally responsible for the continuing review of the organization's financial data, its accounting controls, and for communicating with the staff responsible for preparing financial statements and maintaining internal financial controls. The committee normally reviews audit results, including the review of management's financial performance, and recommends the hiring and firing of auditors.

By affording financial staff access to independent board members, the committee reinforces the independence of outside auditors and guarantees the integrity of the entire audit process, permitting the early identification of troublesome issues. Obviously, the nature of each of its specific tasks depends on the size and complexity of a particular organization.[28]

In some organizations, audit functions are performed by a budget or finance committee, which also is responsible for financial matters generally, such as the review, approval and monitoring of the budget. While this is acceptable, particularly with a smaller board or organization, such a practice should be avoided if it will impair the integrity of the audit process. Audit committee members always should have an opportunity to meet with the organization's auditors without the presence of any staff.

The nominating committee also fulfills an important oversight function by assuring a selection process for board members, the chief staff officer, and, in some cases, other senior staff, independent of those ultimately responsible for management. While the chief staff officer may participate actively in recruiting prospective board members, this officer should not be involved directly in the deliberations of the nominating committee. Independent directors then can be freer to act on a completely disinterested basis, uninfluenced by the presence of a chief staff officer. For similar reasons, other nominating committee functions may include the appointment and assignment of board members to committees and, if the organization does not have a sepa-

11

rate compensation committee, the review and determination of the salaries of the chief staff officer and other senior staff.[29]

Most nonprofit organizations possessing substantial investment assets will have a specific committee whose responsibility it is to supervise the investment of the organization's assets. While boards of smaller organizations still may choose to manage such investments by themselves, under the direction of either the full board or a committee, many organizations today select professional managers and advisers to perform the vital investment research function and make recommendations, either to an investment committee or the board as a whole (some major institutions—Harvard University and the Ford Foundation, for example—have created their own investment management concerns). In the investment area, any constraints on the board's ability to delegate its responsibility to a committee without increasing its exposure to charges of mismanagement if anything goes wrong have largely disappeared as the result of the widespread adoption of the Uniform Management of Institutional Funds Act. The act resolves uncertainties over the ability of nonprofit boards to delegate day-to-day investment management to board committees and independent investment advisers without having to establish in a particular case that such delegation met the requisite standards of conduct.[30]

It is helpful to involve full-time staff in the activities of the particular committee overseeing their area of staff responsibility. The director of development meets with the fundraising committee when it assembles, and the organization's comptroller attends the audit committee meetings. Organizations with an active membership or with a large cadre of committed volunteers also may want to consider including nondirector volunteers on board committees in a nonvoting capacity. This can help stretch board resources, serve as a tool for potential board recruits, and enhance the commitment of volunteers.

A primary goal of the use of committees is the creation and maintenance of a system to assure the regular flow of information to the board, adequate for the board to fulfill its responsibilities on an informed basis. Without timely, accurate, and full information—whether on the credentials and potential conflicts of board candidates, the adequacy of an organization's internal financial controls, or an organization's projected capital budget—a board cannot meet this basic obligation and will fail in its duties. Committees are a proven way for boards to fulfill their governance function by facilitating sound and informed decision-making and oversight.[31]

Legal Limitations on Committees

The law in some states may limit the ability of boards to deploy committees by limiting both the extent to which directors may delegate work to committees and rely safely on their work.[32] In New York, for example, while business directors can comfortably depend on the work of well-chosen committees and outside counsel, accountants, and other professionals and experts, their nonprofit counterparts are only permitted to rely on the work of outside accountants. This does not necessarily preclude reliance, for example, on lawyers, but it may pose certain risks in defending actions based on such reliance. Fortunately, a number of recent cases have permitted and expanded reliance on experts by trustees whose conduct generally is more circumscribed than directors.[33] And the newer and more progressive state nonprofit statutes embody even more extensive reliance features.[34] The consequence of a restrictive approach in a particular state should not bar appropriate reliance or delegation, but it may increase the risk by denying a director the clear-cut protection of a recognized "safe harbor."

While working within established norms of corporate governance, the unique imperatives of nonprofits tend to determine distinctive board attributes: size, independence, voluntary service as well as the basic oversight responsibilities. This organizational structure balances the need for a large, broadly representative board with the effective use of board committees and the reliance on officers and experts to enhance board capability. The prevailing rules are generally supportive of this structure, although there remain some legal limitations on its use.

Chapter 3

WHAT NONPROFIT BOARDS DO

Most writing on board duties deals with evaluating the conduct of directors and does not describe what directors actually do.[1] However it is still possible to assemble a fairly complete picture of board functions from a variety of legal and other sources.

Nonprofit board functions are best understood when divided into two groups: the management of the organization's day-to-day operations (the "internal" management functions) and those that relate to the organization's support, financial and otherwise, from the larger community (the "external" management functions).

Internal Management Functions

The internal functions of the board include establishing operating procedures, budgets and fiscal controls; approving long-range plans; modifying or clarifying the organization's mission; monitoring the performance of the chief staff officer and senior staff; and dealing with matters of succession for directors of self-perpetuating boards as well as for senior staff. These functions derive from statutory and other broadly recognized legal authority (see the section on "Legal Theory versus Board Reality" below).

These internal functions parallel those performed by the directors of business corporations: succession, oversight, decision making, and other legally required tasks.[2] Succession involves the selection, evaluation, and replacement or removal of the executive director and, for larger organizations, other key employees.[3] The oversight function ensures that the organization is being managed consistently with its objectives (its mission) and within its financial resources. (The latter involves not only the periodic review of financial statements, budgets, projections and resource planning, but also the measurement of program efforts and accomplishments.[4] Decision making calls for approving major plans, commitments, and actions (for example, new program initiatives or major modifications of existing programs, resource acquisition or disposition, and new revenue-generating measures, whether a conventional fund-raising drive or a venture into a "nonprofit enterprise"). Other tasks are those specific responsibilities that devolve upon boards, usually by state law or an organization's bylaws (for example, approval of a routine amendment to a corporate charter or the filing of a required report with a state agency) or past practice.[5]

Nonprofit and business directors and their boards share many important characteristics. While some nonprofit directors are relatively inactive, both nonprofit board members and their business colleagues typically devote substantial time to their duties; they perform many similar or, at least, comparable functions; and their ability to deal with nonroutine matters is greatly circumscribed by the dynamics of the meeting process.[6] Like the agenda for a business board, a substantial part of the agenda for a typical nonprofit board (or committee) meeting would be occupied by staff or management reports, routine housekeeping matters (for example, the adoption of banking resolutions), and other concerns dictated by the calendar (the review of annual financial statements, the election of directors and officers, budgeting, required governmental filings, etc.). The balance of a meeting might be devoted to dealing with a limited number of substantive matters (*at most*, one or two).[7]

This probably means that no more than a handful or two of substantive new items are considered each year by the board for action. Some of the matters examined will neither evoke sustained discussion or debate nor touch any fundamental concern.[8] However nonprofit boards tend to be more active than business boards in initiating agenda items and exercising independence in agenda-setting.

While this description holds for large and long-established nonprofit agencies, smaller organizations are likely to have many more pressing issues to contend with, including such fundamental matters as obtaining adequate financial resources (not a frequent concern of business directors), and defining and safeguarding the organization's mission.

External Management Functions

The external functions of a nonprofit board—fund-raising and representing the organization to its surrounding community and any special constituency—are unique to the nonprofit sector.[9]

Fund-raising includes encouraging direct gifts by board members; facilitating government, corporation, and foundation funding; procuring needed goods and services on favorable terms; and providing access to pools of volunteers.

Representing the organization covers the more formal aspects of public relations, such as acting as spokesperson for an institution, as well as participating directly in programs to encourage greater public awareness of an organization and its mission, resolving problems with government agencies, etc. The large size of many nonprofit boards often reflects a number of constituencies and maximizes their representative function through direct board participation and responsibility.

Legal Theory versus Board Reality

What directors actually do matters even if their actions are not reflected explicitly in the law's commands. Most laws governing nonprofit corporations exclusively, are strongly suggestive of the range and extent of conventional directorial duties and responsibilities (see "Internal Management Functions"). Whether the formulation of directors' duties requires that directors manage the corporation as, for example, New York does, or that, as in Delaware and California, the affairs of the corporation may be *managed under the board's direction*, there can be little doubt that directors today, except, perhaps, in new or developing or very small organizations, do not actually manage their organizations' activities, but, rather, superintend their management by others.[10]

In New York, for example, the board is free—because typically there are no members—to adopt or modify the basic governing instruments (the charter and by-laws); the board must deliberate on every fundamental change in organizational character (sales of assets, mergers/consolidations, dissolution); it may appoint, remove, and compensate officers and provide for their duties; it must deal with critical issues of financing such as the issuance of securities; it supervises the investment of corporate funds; it chooses its own successors; it may, under some circumstances, authorize transactions involving conflicts of interests; it may provide for indemnification of officers and directors by the corporation; and, it must monitor the conduct of fellow directors through the ability to remove them and initiate court action challenging their conduct.[11]

Although this list of specific duties is not exhaustive, it is entirely consistent with prevailing legal notions of the two key roles of directors: decision making and oversight. Both functions are included specifically in most nonprofit statutes: responsibility for major corporate decisions (for example, mergers, asset sales, etc.) and clear supervisory authority over officers (appointment, removal, and compensation).[12] Short of identifying the almost limitless variety of major decisions that might come before a board, it is difficult to see how the statutes could be anything but a general guide.

The only shortcoming of nonprofit corporate laws is their failure to address directly the external responsibilities of nonprofit directors.[13] The board's financial responsibilities and the function that volunteer directors perform in representing nonprofits in various situations are central to any portrait of board tasks.[14] Although not explicitly provided for by most nonprofit corporation laws, board responsibility for these two areas is consistent with the broad legal authority directors are given.

Officers and Staff

Unlike most business organizations, the role of chief executive officer in nonprofits is generally bifurcated; there is both a board chair (typically a volunteer director) and a chief operating officer (a full-time staff/program director). The chair often will possess unusual authority, in conjunction with the chief staff officer, to set the agenda and thereby determine what matters to bring before the full board.[15] In large institutions, serving as chair may be virtually a full-time commitment. On the other hand, unlike business organizations, officers (vice presidents, the secretary, the treasurer, etc.) do not manage the organization. Nonprofit officers generally are volunteer directors whose titles are nominal; paid staff actually manage the organization and are not directors.[16]

With two important exceptions, nonprofit boards perform functions that are accurately reflected in the legal norms defining directors' roles. The exceptions—the external functions of fund-raising and representing the organization—have not been fully integrated into the prevailing legal model, although they are functions as central to boards' duty as the others that are commonly recognized. Other board functions, however, are amply supported by legal precedent and even these external functions receive some tacit blessing from the courts.

Chapter 4

THE RESPONSIBILITIES
OF DIRECTORS

We now have an idea of what nonprofit boards look like, how they are structured, and what directors actually do. What then are the legal standards by which the states and their courts evaluate the performance of directors in carrying out their prescribed functions? These legal standards are what are commonly referred to as the "duties" of directors and officers.

How the Law Expects Directors to Act

Nonprofit directors have three commonly recognized duties to the organizations they serve: the duties of care, loyalty, and obedience.[1] The duty of care concerns the director's competence in performing directorial functions and typically requires him to use the "care that an ordinarily prudent person would exercise in a like position and under similar circumstances." The duty of loyalty requires the director's faithful pursuit of the interests of the organization he serves rather than the financial or other interests of the director or of another person or organization. And the duty of obedience requires that a director act with fidelity, within the bounds of the law generally, to the organization's "mission," as expressed in its charter and by-laws.

21

Each of these duties is a duty to the organization only and may be enforced by the organization or by someone (for example, a member or a director) acting on its behalf, whose legal right to enforce such duties derives from the organization's right to do so (thus, such lawsuits are called "derivative" suits). How the breach of these duties may give rise to liability on the part of directors is discussed in the succeeding chapter, "When Directors Get Sued."

The Duty of Care

There probably has been more attention lavished on the content and scope of the duty of care, including the corollary "business judgment rule," than on any other single corporate governance issue. However, after years of debate on this matter, there now is broad agreement on the content of the standards to be applied.[2] Recently a number of states have passed laws that affect the consequences of a breach of that duty and these important changes are discussed in chapter 5.

The Applicable Standard of Care

At one time, the nonprofit community debated whether to apply trust or corporate standards of conduct to nonprofit directors. Among the important differences between the two are: trustees' liability for simple negligence in performing their duties in contrast to directors' enjoyment of the protection of the business judgment rule, making them effectively liable only for gross negligence; the absolute ban on self-dealing by trustees while directors, subject to certain safeguards, may engage in transactions involving conflicting interests; and the nondelegability of trustee's duties, as contrasted to directors' latitude in the same respect.[3] As nonprofit practice was shifting from the frequent application of trust standards (to both trustees of charitable trusts and directors of charitable corporations) to the application of corporate standards, there was a vigorous debate about the relative merits of the two approaches.[4]

Today, the standard of care that is applied to the performance by nonprofit directors of their duties is the corporate standard.[5] The same standard is reflected both in the various states' nonprofit statutes and in judicial decisions. Twenty states have statutory standards of care specifically for nonprofit corporations (as contrasted with thirty-two states with similar statutes for business corporations). Of those twenty, six reflect a standard that requires directors to employ that

> . . . care that an ordinarily prudent person would exercise in a like position and under similar circumstances.[6]

Ten other states have adopted Section 35 of the Model Business Corporation Act, which provides:

> A director shall perform his duties as a director, including his duties as a member of any committee of the board upon which he may serve, in good faith, in a manner he reasonably believes to be in the best interests of the corporation, and with such care as an ordinarily prudent person in a like position would use under similar circumstances.[7]

And, one requires directors to act

> . . . in the best interests of the corporation, and with such care, including reasonable inquiry, as is appropriate under the circumstances.[8]

The balance of the states have neither explicit statutory nor definitive common law standards governing nonprofit directors.[9]

The basic statutory version of the applicable standard of conduct is echoed in the few court cases that have dealt with duty of care issues independently of issues of self-dealing by directors. There are only a handful of these cases, and the decisions in all but one espouse a corporate standard, although they span almost fifty years and emanate from different jurisdictions.[10] These few cases deal with issues such as losses on investments, the breadth of investment authority, and the propriety of compensation to staff or advisers. Only one case (from California) imposes any liability on directors based on a trust standard.[11] Given the facts of that case (the retention of substantial funds in a noninterest bearing account for five years), it is unlikely that any different result would have been reached whatever standard was employed.[12]

What the Duty of Care Means

In examining in detail the meaning of the duty of care, we will examine the statutory duty of care proposed by the Revised Model Nonprofit Corporation Act (RMNCA). More comprehensive than most formulations, it contains virtually every element of the various existing statutes and case law.

The RMNCA duty of care provision is as follows:

Section 8.30 GENERAL STANDARDS FOR DIRECTORS

(a) A director shall discharge his or her duties as a director, including his or her duties as a member of a committee:

    (1) in good faith;

    (2) with the care an ordinarily prudent person in a like position would exercise under similar circumstances; and

    (3) in a manner the director reasonably believes to be in the best interests of the corporation.

(b) In discharging his or her duties a director is entitled to rely on information, opinions, reports, or statements, including financial statements and other financial data, if prepared or presented by:

    (1) one or more officers or employees of the corporation whom the director reasonably believes to be reliable and competent in the matters presented;

    (2) legal counsel, public accountants or other persons as to matters the director reasonably believes are within the person's professional or expert competence; or

    (3) a committee of the board of which the director is not a member, as to matters within its jurisdiction, if the director reasonably believes the committee merits confidence.

    (c) A director is not acting in good faith if the director has knowledge concerning the matter in question that makes reliance otherwise permitted by subsection (b) unwarranted.

    (d) A director is not liable for the performance of the duties of his or her office if the director acted in compliance with this section.

The meaning of this section of the RMNCA is made clearer by a discussion of several of its crucial terms.

Good Faith—Directors must act in good faith. This means essentially what it does in common speech: honesty of intention, openness, and fair dealing. Because the concept of good faith incorporates a large element of unverifiable subjective intention, professions of "good faith" might be suspect. Therefore, the law looks to some objective means of assessing its presence. For example, a group of physicians was accused of a conflict of interest in selling a proprietary hospital to a nonprofit association on terms arguably favorable to their personal interests, while simultaneously retaining control of a profitable private practice formerly affiliated with the institution. However, the court noted as evidence of the physicians' good faith, that the doctors had forgiven substantial payments owed to them by the nonprofit hospital from the original sale.[13] In the court's view, the doctors' willingness, in effect, to return part of the purchase price to which they were legally entitled, supported their position that the original sale was fair. However, when good faith is mere rhetoric, unaccompanied by any visible acts courts tend to be more skeptical.[14]

Best Interests—This signifies the need for directors to act, not in their personal interests or even the interests of others, but, rather, in the interests of the organization they are serving. It is discussed more fully under the "Duty of Loyalty."

Ordinarily Prudent Person—This phrase connotes two distinct concepts. One is that of ordinariness—not in the sense of mediocrity but in the sense of possessing no special skills or technical expertise.

Directors, in the law's eyes, are generalists (that does not mean that specialists do not have their place on a board nor that a specialist may not have to use his special learning). Ordinary prudence means that directors are expected to possess and exercise sound, practical judgment, to employ common sense, and to reach sound, informed conclusions (although the conclusions they reach need not be the right ones). Directors, acting as ordinarily prudent persons, do not, thereby, guarantee the success of investments or activities, programs, or grants.[15] And prudence is not to be equated with excessive caution, whether in making investment or programmatic decisions.

Care—The concept of care incorporates a number of related ideas. Directors should be diligent and attentive. "Diligence" implies an active interest in the organization's activities. A director who attended few or no meetings, read no materials, and was otherwise uninvolved would not manifest the requisite diligence. Directors must spend enough time on the organization's affairs to be reasonably acquainted with matters demanding their attention. Such attention ordinarily requires informed attendance at meetings, including the review and comprehension of any materials submitted to the board.[16]

"Attention" involves directors evaluating such things as potential problems, their magnitude, the general situation of the organization at the time, and the extent to which committees, experts, and others are relied on—formally or informally. Attention may involve inquiry into particular matters when information or its lack raises some issue of concern that doesn't seem to be properly addressed. For example, the failure to deal with a shortcoming noted in an auditor's management review letter could be deemed critical, sustaining a finding of inattention and, hence, a violation of the duty of care leading to liability. While sustained inattention or unreasonable blindness will lead to liability, attentiveness need not be equated with needless questioning for the sake of appearances. Thus, for example, the time and cost of acquiring information may properly be balanced against the urgency of a decision.[17]

In a Like Position, Under Similar Circumstances—The standard of care expected of directors is always a flexible one, adapted to the realities of varied situations. Thus, "in a like position" means that directors' conduct is measured with respect to that unique corporation they are serving, recognizing that different organizations have different goals, objectives, and resources. "In a like position" connotes an evaluation based on facts at the time a decision is made, as well as distinctions among directors. While the law is premised on the generalist director, it also takes into account the greater knowledge of the organization that an "insider" may have or, for example, the special skills a banker possesses in evaluating a loan transaction.

"Under similar circumstances" reflects the distinctive settings in which nonprofit directors make decisions. For example, the standard of care may be applied in a way that reflects the unique functions nonprofit directors perform by way of fund-raising as well as their uncompensated service.[18] However, the standard requires all board members to be functioning directors; allowances are not made for a nominal director (for example, one whose only involvement consisted of making a single large donation each year).[19]

Although employee-directors tend to be relatively uncommon in nonprofit organizations, they should be expected to have a greater awareness of the organization's activities and should be expected to play an active role in monitoring, problem-solving, and decision making.[20] Although their greater knowledge may entail a heavier legal obligation for employee-directors, they, too, should be permitted to rely on fellow officers or other experts.[21]

The phrase "under similar circumstances" also involves considerations of the particular size and complexity of an organization, the urgency of a decision, potential risks (and rewards), and the information available at the time a decision is made. For example, evaluating a proposed transaction on the basis of incomplete information may be appropriate if the opportunity is time-limited and could confer substantial benefits on an organization. Or, a relatively modest proposal for a new fund-raising concept might require less scrutiny than one with substantially greater cost.

Reliance and Delegation—Although a number of statutes and court decisions distinguish between board "reliance" on others for information and opinion and board "delegation" of functions, there is no meaningful conceptual difference. Both result from the need of boards to use others to aid in performing their duties responsibly. Directors may not abdicate their responsibilities and be relieved of potential liability simply by relying blindly on others or by delegating authority to board committees, officers, or other agents of the organization (for example, employees or outside experts). Directors must comply with the general standards of care in the selection and ongoing surveillance of those on whom they have either relied for information or to whom they have delegated board power or authority. Factors to be considered in evaluating the care involved in any such reliance or delegation include the knowledge the director has regarding a particular matter when making the assignment, his appraisal of the capabilities and diligence of the board committees, officers, or others and the relative importance of the issue to the organization.

Primarily because of the large size of the average nonprofit board, delegating the performance of critical functions to committees is inevitable for the effective discharge of a board's responsibilities.[22] Directors are entitled to assume that delegated activities are being carried out responsibly (unless, they know or should know otherwise). If the directors have acted properly in delegating, courts will not hold them liable for the actions or omissions of those to whom such delegated responsibilities have been assigned. This protection applies to all actions that boards aren't otherwise barred from delegating, including those choices a board makes in determining what matters to consider (for example, delegating formally or informally to the chair and executive director the construction of the agenda for board meetings).[23]

Directors actually serving on a committee are subject to the basic "prudent person" standard of care in carrying out their committee assignments. Under the RMNCA formula, a committee must act in a way to merit the confidence of the board if the board's reliance on the committee is to be proper. To "merit confidence," however, does not mean that committee members need any special "expertise" or skills (unlike experts—lawyers, accountants, or others), although committee action must be informed by expert opinion when technical subjects are being deliberated. A board, therefore, may rely on a report by a board committee concerning a prospective capital improvement, although no committee member has technical expertise in the area. On the other hand, it could not rely on an "expert" who lacked special skills or knowledge. For example, the board would be unjustified if it relied on a lawyer specializing in copyright law to evaluate the legal implications of a complex real estate transaction.

Reliance, to be effective, requires vigilance by the board so that material or advice relied on forms the basis of an informed judgment. In other words, a report must have been read, thought about, listened to, or otherwise assimilated and digested. A director can't properly rely upon a fund-raising consultant's report if all the director knows is the report's conclusion—that would not be acting in "good faith" nor would it give sufficient means to evaluate the expert's performance. For example, merely knowing that an expert is regarded widely as competent generally would not excuse a lack of familiarity with a report demonstrating technical incompetence or egregious bad judgment. In most circumstances a director is entitled to rely on reports prepared by individuals or committees (assuming that their contents have been absorbed); where a director has a reasonable basis to be suspicious, the general duty of care requires the director to make further inquiry.

The fact that directors and officers act as a group has important practical and legal implications. Being informed, in addition to drawing on his own background, may mean relying on the discussions of other directors and on staff reports. For example, a director is recognized as an expert in a specific area, fellow board members may give greater weight to his views within that area. Equally important to reliance on other directors may be their different backgrounds, the dynamics of collective action (the distinct role each director plays in the organization, the value of maintaining board cohesiveness, or the importance of sustaining the morale of senior staff), the magnitude of the matter under consideration, the time frame in which a decision must be made, and similar factors. All determine whether a director is informed about the subject of his judgment. This is all the duty of care requires. A director need not exhaustively research every issue personally to comply with the legal requisites.[24]

Legal Limits on Reliance and Delegation

State laws differ widely on the authority of boards of directors to make extensive use of committees, and of senior staff and the board to delegate extensively to well-qualified and properly chosen experts—accountants, lawyers, engineers, fund-raising counsel, or others.[25] In New York, for example, directors may only rely on financial statements prepared by auditors and the performance by others of investment responsibilities (so long as the requisite standard of conduct is employed in delegating such functions).[26] In contrast, California permits reliance on a host of experts as well as committees so long as the reliance is justified.[27] As discussed in chapter 2, a board is not prevented by these statutory restrictions from relying on others or delegating their power to act, but the susceptibility of such conduct to a legal challenge is greater in those states without generous "safe harbor" provisions like California (or the RMNCA).

Special Nonprofit Considerations

Many charities have large boards because board membership usually entails making a substantial contribution. While some directors may exercise their responsibilities with vigilance, others, serving primarily by virtue of their financial capacity, will neither be inclined, nor able, to carry out their duties adequately. The law, however, does not distinguish among these types of directors. All are subject to the same duties; all are potentially subject to the same liabilities.[28]

Nevertheless, such board service, almost always gratuitous and frequently involving substantial commitments of time and money, is a widespread phenomenon in the nonprofit world and may account for the implicit sympathy with which courts seem to view the conduct of directors when challenged, at least when no conflicting interest is present.[29] However, until the law clearly recognizes this legitimate need of nonprofit organizations, nonprofits should strive to avoid the dilemma of the passive donor/director by finding or creating suitable alternatives for recognizing and rewarding individual service and generosity.[30]

Case Studies from the Real World

Each of the following case histories is derived from real events, modified to emphasize particular issues concerning the duty of care and related business judgment rule, the duty of loyalty and the duty of obedience.* But, like the real situations, these cases do not come packaged with labels reading "Duty of Loyalty" or "Duty of Care," but rather involve complex events, multiple issues, distinct personalities, and all the other features of real life. After a full presentation of the facts of each case, there follows an analysis of the legal doctrines involved, the application of those legal issues to the specific facts in the example, and an appraisal of the directors' and officers' actions, together with commentary about desirable practice in handling related issues. The case studies have been incorporated into this chapter because, while they do touch on matters of liability and indemnification and insurance, subjects covered in the two final chapters, they are concerned primarily with issues relating to the content of directors' duties and only secondarily with the consequences of their violation.

Case Studies: the Duty of Care

The Passive Director: Inattention and the Duty of Care

The Community Arts Association (CAA) is a publicly supported performing arts organization that operates a community theater, a local symphony, and a number of educational programs in the performing arts for children and adults. Forty percent of its annual $4 million budget derives from direct and indirect government support, and the balance comes from corporate and foundation support, individual contributions, and program revenues, including ticket sales. The board consists of thirty persons, composed of arts professionals, academics, local civic leaders, business people, etc. Some directors are very familiar with CAA's program and the services that CAA offers. Others have management and/or financial planning expertise but con-

---

*The names and other characteristics of all real persons and institutions also have been changed.

siderably less familiarity with the programs it offers; still others are donors who otherwise are uninvolved in the board's deliberations. The board meets four times yearly. Materials are rarely furnished in advance of meetings except for minutes from the preceding board meeting and a sparse agenda. Financial and other reports are distributed at meetings on an irregular schedule.

CAA operates its major program out of an aging and no longer adequate facility. One of the directors has learned of an opportunity to purchase a building that could be converted into a suitable performing arts center. The offering price is $700,000, and an additional $350,000 will be necessary to renovate the building to make it suitable for CAA's special needs. The renovated building could then house virtually all of the organization's programs as well as its executive offices.

This proposed purchase is presented to the board at a regular meeting by the group's executive director (who is not a board member but attends all meetings). The executive director, while an experienced and capable arts administrator and highly knowledgeable about the organization's finances and programs, has little experience in real estate transactions, valuation, construction, or management. CAA's property manager did not inspect the building prior to board action. The consideration of this issue by the board evokes no dissent and little discussion. The board approves the purchase and authorizes the executive director to complete the transaction, based on the $1,050,000 total cost of the transaction and CAA's perceived need.

Six months after the purchase of the new facility, CAA had trouble meeting its obligation to pay the purchase money mortgage held by the seller (which had a variable interest rate that rose two percentage points during the year). There were substantial cost overruns in renovating the new building. One year after the purchase, CAA filed a voluntary petition in bankruptcy. During the bankruptcy proceedings, it was disclosed that the individual from whom CAA had bought the building had himself purchased it just one year earlier at a cost of only $140,000.

The key issue here is the extent to which the board informed itself before authorizing the commitment of the organization's resources for a major capital investment. There is a substantial likelihood that, had the organization possessed more complete information concerning the facility, it could have acquired it at a significantly reduced cost. Even a 100 percent profit for the seller would have cost CAA only $280,000, a savings of more than $400,000 from the purchase price—a sizable sum for an organization with a $4 million budget.

The board's seeming indifference to the importance of the transaction might be looked at differently if this had been merely one of many similar transactions being handled pursuant to a well-established procedure (in which case the board need not have focused closely on specifics). That, however, is hardly the case here. The board should have appreciated the significance of the proposed transaction and taken reasonable steps to inform itself of the relevant facts so negotiation of the terms of the transaction by CAA might occur on a fully informed basis and be as advantageous as possible to CAA's interests.

The valuation of real property is a complex technical matter, one certainly beyond the expected skills of directors. The board could have fulfilled its responsibility by relying on officers, employees, experts, or others who reasonably could have assembled and evaluated the pertinent information competently. They could have done this by retaining experts and creating a committee to report back to the full board with a recommendation for action, based on its evaluation of expert opinion.

The directors here, however, did nothing. While informal reliance on officers may be perfectly proper if it is part of an accepted or considered way of doing business, when dealing with a situation not previously faced, it would seem unwise. Although the transaction involved no "suspicious circumstances" (there was no relationship between the seller and any CAA board member), it was a sufficiently important undertaking (a major, virtually unique decision) for the directors to have made some inquiry into the terms. Here, no experts were employed; not even CAA's own property manager inspected the building until the contract was signed and, then, only with a view to ascertaining its structural integrity and not to estimating the accuracy of the projected renovation costs.

Thus, even the minimal requisites of the business judgment rule were not complied with by the board in authorizing the building's purchase. Although the decision by the board was made in good faith, involved no conflicting interests and, arguably, was "rational" (i.e., the charity legitimately needed the facility, which was passingly suitable for its purpose), it was not an informed decision. In such a case, the business judgment rule, even if applied, affords no protection to the board from possible liability (there is a fuller discussion of the business judgment rule in the next section of this chapter).

While, under duty of care standards, such passivity may have been acceptable if the board was reasonable in its reliance on others better qualified technically to evaluate such decisions, the unusual size and significance of the transaction should have alerted the board to the need for some independent scrutiny. Here, there was none, nor did the board rely on recognized experts.

Furthermore, the board could not justify its handling of this matter without establishing that it took sufficient time to deliberate adequately and review relevant information. Although, in the interests of efficiency and in light of the realities of the burdens of volunteering, the board may be able to conduct much of its regular business informally, with a minimum of "paper," a significant action like the purchase could not be adequately presented to an unprepared board on the basis of cursory information and no written record.

In this example, the directors and the executive director who, if considered an officer, would be subject to at least as great a duty of care as the directors (if not greater) by virtue of his heightened familiarity with CAA's activities, have breached the duty of care to CAA.[31] Nevertheless, the identification of a breach of duty is not tantamount to a finding of liability. It is far from clear that this unwise board decision alone, however egregious, led to CAA's ultimate bankruptcy. Here, numerous and complex factors leading to CAA's eventual insolvency, of which the imprudent purchase was merely one, would all have to be examined. At the same time, if some loss or injury to CAA could be demonstrated (for example, if it is shown that CAA overpaid because of the board's mishandling of the transaction), liability for that harm to CAA could be imposed on the directors in the context of the bankruptcy proceeding or by other independent legal action.*

---

*The discussion of liability, legal indemnification, and directors' and officers' insurance which takes up the balance of this case study is included for

Were the court to find breach of duty, it then would have to determine whether each director or officer bore equal responsibility for such breach. Like many such publicly supported charities, CAA has a diverse board. While the directors may bring different abilities to the board and represent differing interests and constituencies, they are uniformly held to the same standards of conduct. That a particular director, who serves only because he has generously supported the organization over the years, is unable or unwilling to fulfill his oversight responsibilities as a board member makes no difference in assessing his ultimate liability.[32]

Who bears the expense if liability has been imposed, resulting from court action by a state attorney general, for example, or if there has been an expensive and costly investigation into the board's role? Under most indemnification statutes, CAA, in these circumstances, would be entitled to indemnify its directors at the outset of any such proceeding. Mandatory indemnification, on the other hand, is typically available only where a director has been vindicated or where a court, in other circumstances, orders indemnification. In this case, at the commencement of the investigative process, both CAA and its directors would need to consult separate legal counsel because of their potentially conflicting interests (because the directors might be determined to have caused the harm to CAA). Here the directors would only be indemnified for their expenses if CAA, by virtue of a provision in its charter or by-laws, or by specific action of the board, had undertaken to indemnify directors generally or did so in this particular case. Precisely because of the discretion vested in the board to decide whether or not to indemnify a director and to advance the legal expenses of defending a lawsuit or carrying out an investigation (and especially where, unlike this example, not all directors are at equal risk of suit), independent indemnification contracts can be particularly valuable to directors seeking assured protection.

In the usual case, of course, the director(s) being sued will want their legal expenses paid from the outset. To do that, under most

---

purposes of providing a complete example. The legal issues relating to these subjects are discussed in detail in chapters 5 and 6 and the reader may want to return to this example after reviewing that material.

statutes, some disinterested decision maker—the board, a committee of the board, members (there are none here), or "special counsel"— would have to determine that the director(s) seeking the indemnity had met an applicable standard of conduct. While this does not usually involve a board determination that the director(s) adhered to the duty of care, a finding that the director acted in the organization's interests and in good faith is usually required.

Here, it is likely that the conduct of all directors would be challenged. Therefore, neither the full board nor a board committee would possess the necessary disinterestedness to make the required decision on advancing expenses; a special counsel, appointed by the full board, would have to decide.*

The propriety of paying defense counsel for the directors and, ultimately, indemnifying directors for any liabilities incurred depends on the way in which the conduct of the board was challenged. In a derivative lawsuit, one brought primarily for CAA's benefit, expenses could not be advanced nor indemnity granted without court approval and only then, if the director seeking the indemnification is found not to have been liable for or, in some cases, committed a breach of his duty to the organization.** For example, a derivative-type action by the state's attorney general, at least past the investigative stage, would make any indemnity of little value, even to the extent of precluding advancement of expenses.[33]

In contrast, in an action brought by third parties, the law is considerably more generous. An action by, for example, financial patrons of CAA, if allowed to bring suit, would permit the indemnification of directors, including the advance of expenses, as long as the directors had been acting in good faith and in the best interests of CAA.

This discussion points up the shortcomings of indemnification schemes; they are most precarious just in those instances when most

---

*Delaware, Pennsylvania, New York, and some other states no longer require a case-by-case determination of eligibility for advancement of expenses and organizations may authorize general procedures for advancing expenses.

**Again, some of the recent legislation now permits indemnification in derivative suits (except those involving a breach of the duty of loyalty).

needed. That is why prudence dictates that directors' and officers' (D & O) liability insurance be procured; it protects both the organization's obligation to indemnify its directors by backing up corporate promises with insurance dollars and it independently protects directors in many cases when the corporation cannot provide indemnification under the prevailing law. In the case of CAA, an insurance policy would cover the expenses incurred by all directors in defending an action against them based on their alleged misconduct so long as no self-dealing was involved. The insurance coverage afforded in derivative-type claims, except for self-dealing, is one of the great virtues of D&O coverage. Here, it would fully protect all directors and officers because only duty of care issues are implicated and no conflicts of interest exist.[34]

Under Delaware law, which now permits a "cap" on liability or its complete elimination for duty of care violations, and under the law of other states, like Pennsylvania, that now permit indemnification even in derivative-type actions not involving self-dealing or reckless or willful misconduct, the foregoing analysis would yield results even more favorable to directors (although not necessarily to the executive director, who is a paid officer).

The Faithless Officer: The Limits of Delegation and the Duty of Care

In 1972, Bill Promoter, a former professional wrestling impresario and producer of "variety shows," organized a charitable corporation for the primary purpose of furnishing direct assistance to patients suffering from chronic eating disorders (the "Association"). Of organizations serving this constituency, only the Association actually assisted the victims of this group of ailments rather than focusing on research. To build a financial base, the Association carried on extensive direct-mail fund-raising. To give the group some initial legitimacy, Promoter filled its board with prominent physicians, research scientists, and other health professionals familiar with these related disorders.

After a couple of years of apparently steady but unspectacular growth in financial support gained primarily through its direct-mail campaigns, Promoter came under the scrutiny of the Internal Revenue

Service, which, in the course of a routine audit, had determined that a majority of the Association's revenues were paid either to him for his services as executive director or to vendors, contractors, and other third parties with whom he had a variety of preexisting business, professional, and personal relationships. Facing charges of private gain, the Association agreed to a thorough-going reorganization, and Promoter resigned his position with the Association and severed all other ties with it. A number of directors, including Promoter's cronies, also resigned from the board. The remaining directors, however, decided to continue to serve the organization.

The Association's board then hired a new executive director who had formerly been employed by a professional fund-raising firm, although he lacked any knowledge of, or experience with, eating disorders and health issues generally. However, the board concluded that, given the Association's dependence on direct-mail fund-raising, it was vital to have a director with extensive fund-raising experience to assure the Association's continued financial vitality. They also concluded that the recent debacle had been caused by the virtual absence of internal financial controls. Although the staff numbered only six, they hired a full-time, experienced bookkeeper and engaged the services of an independent public accounting firm to conduct an annual audit and a related management review that would include an annual assessment of the Association's financial practices.

During the ensuing decade, the Association prospered: its revenues increased tenfold, its staff quintupled, its programs, while still modest in comparison to the well-known health industry giants, increased dramatically and received wide approbation. As the executive director became increasingly occupied with the public aspects of leading a national organization, with its frequent travel, conferences, and the like, he turned over much of the operational management to the associate director, who was hired in 1979 and who had performed as an able and efficient manager, complementing the executive director's fund-raising and other "public" skills.

In early 1984, in the course of a routine audit, Bead, Counter & Co. discovered unmistakable evidence of a substantial diversion of funds by the associate director for her own use, principally through the use of false invoices with "friendly suppliers" and other contractors who shared in the profits of her scheme.

After this was called to the board's attention, it acted quickly, firing the associate director, seeking restitution from her, and employing special counsel to investigate the matter thoroughly. The Association also recovered fully its claim under a fidelity bond insuring it against acts of employee dishonesty. That investigation led to a number of salutary reforms within the organization, including enhanced internal financial controls and the hiring of a chief financial officer (the organization had been without one for some time; the occasionally temperamental executive director had dismissed the last one two years earlier).

After these matters were reported in the ordinary course of events to various state regulatory authorities, the attorney general of the state where the Association is headquartered began an investigation of the whole affair. On learning that the organization's financial controls were lax and the board met only infrequently, the attorney general decided to sue the Association's directors for negligence.

The liability issue here involved a determination of whether the unfortunate recurrence represented a regrettable—but excusable— flaw, such as might exist with even the most secure financial controls, or constituted a failure of the oversight system itself, indicating that the directors had failed to monitor the activities of the Association properly.

No system of internal financial controls can assure the honesty of every employee, including senior staff, nor the unfailing ability to detect venality. In the wake of the 1974 scandal, the board, at the urging of the IRS, had put in place adequate financial controls, including internal financial staff and an external auditor. The dismissal of the internal comptroller, who had a critical role in assuring the integrity of the financial controls, might, in other circumstances, be cause for alarm. But here, there was nothing surrounding the dismissal of that employee that should have alerted the board. The executive director was well known to be honest and dedicated, if somewhat difficult, and staff turnover was a persistent problem. In fact, the dismissal itself, although it may have opened the way for the imple-

39

mentation of the scheme, could not reasonably have been foreseen as the cause of the diversion, even if the board was somewhat lax in securing a replacement.

Most importantly, the board appropriately relied on Bead, Counter & Co. to audit the Association's financial statements and conduct an annual review for the board of the adequacy of its internal financial controls. This was done each year for nine years. In not one case did the management review letters comment adversely on any aspect of the Association's financial practices or internal controls; all comments were of a routine nature and were responded to promptly.

The board's determination of what internal financial controls are needed is treated by the court like any other board decision. In this case, nothing of a sufficiently suspicious nature had occurred to alert the board to make any unusual inquiry into the adequacy of the financial controls. There is no general obligation to look behind the actions of others on whom boards necessarily and routinely rely.

An examination of invoices to suppliers who were in league with the associate director may have revealed a pattern of fraud, but directors are not expected to perform such tasks, except when they already have been alerted to the existence of a potentially serious problem. Modest increases in functional expenses (for example, a marked but not shocking increase in printing expenses) noted in the course of a board's financial review or budget preparations could be explained quite plausibly (for example, more fund-raising brochures were printed or per-unit costs increased modestly) without reference to massive fraud. Massive fraud is not the explanation that, given the very important presumption of regularity that directors must accord to staff action, would come to mind.

A troubling issue is whether the executive director similarly would escape liability in such a case. The "like position" of the standard of care takes into account that directors and officers are invariably in different positions from one another because of their situation when events occur and because of who they are. A full-time officer, such as the executive director, should be more familiar with the activities of an organization under his direct supervision than those volunteer directors who do not have day-to-day responsibilities. Such potentially enhanced liability could also apply to directors who, by virtue of special committee service or some other assignment, assume special responsibilities and, through such special service acquire particular knowledge. For example, had the Association's annual management review letter from Bead, Counter & Co. noted that the lack of an internal auditor was a critical deficiency in the Association's internal financial controls, then, at the very least, the audit committee members would have been expected to have learned this in carrying out their routine committee responsibilities. In such a case, they would be on notice to make further inquiry. The failure to do so then could lead to liability.

The real issue is not whether this particular fraud should have been detected by the executive director or others. Like most skillful schemes, it probably couldn't have been discovered, except by sheer luck or the most careful review (which, unless the board were alerted to the need for it, would not normally be undertaken simply because of the expense). The executive director, however, was most attuned to the need for a comprehensive system of internal financial controls, given the Association's unfortunate history in this regard and the potentially disastrous impact a recurrence could have on the viability of a scandal-plagued organization dependent on public support. While any officer, including the executive director, is entitled to rely on others, that reliance must be reasonable, and the executive director's virtual abdication of all financial responsibilities, given these circumstances, would make such reliance impermissible precisely because of his greater familiarity with the Association's activities. In this case, although the volunteer directors should be permitted to rely on the audit process, the executive director could not look solely to outside experts in light of his presumed familiarity with all of the Association's affairs.

A more difficult question is whether those who served on the board since the Association's inception are viewed as having greater familiarity with the internal financial controls and the critical position that an internal auditor occupies. Given the passage of time between the two occurrences (almost ten years) and the lack of any problems during that time, the directors (including the original ones) would probably not be regarded as having breached any duty to the Association and should incur no liability. They were entitled to rely on outside experts, the officers, and the committees. Just because some responsibilities of the executive and associate directors were reassigned would not, under ordinary conditions be indicative of problems or of the need to make further inquiry. In practice, such arrangements—an "inside" and "outside" officer—are quite common.

In this case, the directors should incur no expense by virtue of the organization's obligation to indemnify them, assuming it has an indemnification plan (if not, then the directors here could seek and obtain court-awarded indemnification because they violated no duty to the organization). The executive director, having breached his duty of care to the organization, could not be indemnified, but, because no self-dealing was involved, he would be protected from actual loss through a D&O policy if the Association had obtained one.*

Using Experts (and Staff): Reliance and the Duty of Care

The Bison Institute of Arts and Sciences is the premiere cultural institution in Wayne County (pop. 1,600,000). The Institute's principal activity is the operation of an important regional history museum. New Wayne, the county seat (pop. 425,000), is an old manufacturing city with an aging industrial base. For almost twenty years, the city has lost jobs and population to metropolitan Wayne County.

Over the years, middle class and upper middle class patrons of the Institute have flagged in their financial support and the number of visitors has declined. This segment of the community traditionally had provided the Institute with most of its private support, starting around the turn of the century with major gifts and continuing for more than fifty years, during which time the Institute mounted a number of successful building fund and capital campaign drives and amassed a substantial endowment. Most of the funds raised in these campaigns were generated through the personal efforts of the Institute's large and prestigious board—forty-three pillars of the community (the publisher of the Wayne *Gazette,* leading lawyers and physicians, clergymen, bankers, and others of similarly impeccable credentials).

---

*Indemnification and insurance are discussed in detail in chapter 6.

With the drying up of federal funds, adverse tax law changes imminent, and the erosion of much of its traditional support, the Institute expects its small deficits for each of the past three years to increase substantially. While, historically, the Institute's private fund-raising efforts have been highly successful, there is no certainty that they can close the growing gaps now forecast, with the inevitable consequence that services may have to be curtailed and/or endowment depleted. One of the board members has suggested that the Institute retain a marketing consultant to explore the feasibility of developing additional revenues through an aggressive "promotion" of the modest museum store, adding tuition for selected programs, changing the membership fee structure, etc. In support of this recommendation, he discussed examples of revenue-generating activities undertaken by other cultural institutions, which he had read about in newspapers and magazines.

The board, after some resistance to the notion of "marketing" its cultural mission, agreed to refer the matter to its development committee, which had primary responsibility for fund-raising. Eleven of the forty-three board members serve on that committee, although not all committee members attend regularly. The committee's quorum requirement is one-third (four); usually five or six members attend and take final action. The committee meets on an as-needed basis. The Institute's development director who, with a small staff, has traditionally provided administrative services for the Institute's major fund-raising drives and assisted in its planned giving activities, regularly meets with the full board and the development committee, as does the administrator.

The development staff, with the aid of board members, identified a number of marketing consultants. After reviewing resumes, checking references and conducting interviews with the most promising candidates, the staff tentatively recommended one to the committee for its consideration. The committee met and interviewed the candidate for one hour about her experience and plans. It concluded that she was competent and agreed that she would be retained for an initial fee of $25,000 to produce a feasibility study and, subject to board approval, to implement a marketing plan for an additional fee. The full board played no role in the process, and the committee itself relied heavily on the efforts of the development staff and the administrator. These procedures were characteristic of the way the Institute had operated over the years.

After a few months, the consultant produced a report recommending several strategies for introducing and implementing an intensive marketing effort targeted at the suburban population. The principal recommendation was to employ an aggressive direct-mail marketing program aimed at affluent families in the nearer suburbs.

This report and the recommendations were presented to the board by the administrator and development director, after first being circulated to committee members. After presentation of the report and a few pertinent but deferential questions, the board adopted the report and authorized the administrator, the development director, and other staff to implement the recommendations, subject to the continuing oversight of the development committee.

At the end of the first year, the campaign had incurred direct expenses of almost $500,000, while revenues traceable to the campaign were less than $300,000. In reviewing the situation, the consultant stressed the high cost of initial marketing efforts and the time it would take to cultivate this potential constituency to produce substantial revenues. This explanation was accepted by the board. At the end of the second year, although the performance was somewhat better, the campaign still did not net any proceeds, and the cumulative loss had reached $450,000. In her review, the consultant stressed that such campaigns take a minimum of three years before they generally start showing a return and, sometimes, take as long as five years before they generate any substantial income.

Following the third full year of the campaign, the results continued to be disappointing. The campaign lost $150,000, resulting in a three-year cumulative loss of more than $600,000. The consultant's fees now totaled $175,000. The development committee, in reviewing the situation, concluded that the campaign should be terminated and losses minimized.

If the attorney general or a disgruntled director who had remained skeptical about "marketing" a cultural mission brought suit, would the directors be found to have breached their duty of care in relying on the development committee to initiate and oversee the marketing program? Did the directors and/or committee members breach their duty in relying on the technical expertise of the professional consultant and the administrator and development director to evaluate the consultant's plan?

This example focuses on the circumstances in which a board may rely on experts and the extent to which it can delegate its authority to others to evaluate information and make decisions on important matters. Nonprofit directors must rely on information developed or evaluated by others: fellow directors sitting on a committee, officers, staff, and outside experts. Here, the board used all three.[35] This, of course, is consistent with the widely recognized "oversight" model for boards, in which directors do not themselves manage but monitor how others do so.

Given the uncompensated nature of nonprofit service, the time constraints involved in evaluating information, and the size and composition of the typical nonprofit board, reliance by boards on others to evaluate information, make recommendations, and monitor developments is essential. A forty-three person board, particularly if it lacks an individual with relevant experience (here, an expert in cultural resources marketing or, at a minimum, marketing generally) would have to rely on the expertise of others. It could not take the time to accumulate the necessary knowledge and sophistication, even with the most diligent application.

The key to the legitimacy of a board's reliance is its reasonableness. The law confers broad authority on the board to manage the Institute. It recognizes the need of nonprofit boards to appoint officers and staff, define their duties, fix their compensation and the like, and through the adoption of rules for regulating the management of its activities (by-laws), organize the performance of complex functions.

Here, the board practice has been to rely on special or standing committees both (1) to gather information and report back with recommendations and (2) to take action on their own in particular cases. Even if the board reserved the action-taking role for itself, it still would have to rely heavily on a committee to marshal information and evaluate it. The board then would be in the position of having to engage in a more or less perfunctory review of that information and, undoubtedly, would have little real chance but to accept the committee recommendations. It seems acceptable, therefore, to permit the committee itself to have charge both of monitoring the campaign and ultimate decision-making.[36]

The critical issue here was the effectiveness of the board's or committee's evaluation of the competence of the expert. Here, the committee relied on the staff to screen and evaluate candidates, an entirely proper procedure utilizing the critical judgmental faculties of both a staff officer with relevant professional expertise (the development director) and the substantial practical experience and familiarity with the institution of its chief staff officer, a seasoned veteran.[37] In this case, resumes were examined and references were checked. The staff also evaluated fees charged for comparable services and concluded that $25,000 for a feasibility study was at the lower end of the average range for such a study. All of this was reported informally to the committee. Finally, the legally sufficient number of committee members (i.e., a quorum) met and interviewed the candidate. There was no apparent deficiency in this selection process.

And there should be no distinction between relying on an outside expert (the marketing consultant) and an employee-expert (the development director) even if the board can exercise somewhat greater control over the development director. The board still should be able to rely on a properly chosen and monitored outside expert because in most cases organizations, unless they have extremely large and diverse staffs, with a full complement of experts for all contingencies, necessarily have to look to outside experts for assistance.

The next step for analysis by a court assessing the propriety of board action would be a review of the full board's approval of the plan developed by the consultant. The development committee received the consultant's marketing plan well in advance of the full board meeting and had an opportunity to review it, formulate critical questions, and articulate any concerns it had. The balance of the board (the noncommittee members) did not have that opportunity and only saw the report at the board meeting. At the same time, the board already had ceded authority to the committee for developing and implementing a fund-raising strategy. Finally, the Institute's professional staff and administrator, on whom both board and committee implicitly relied, were closely involved during the entire process and raised no substantial objections.

While lawyers like evidence of a robust and vigorous exchange of views as a sign of board compliance with its responsibilities, such behavior is more typical of the courtroom than the boardroom. The reality is more often reflected by our example in the polite but perfunctory questions following the delivery of the consultant's report.[38] In any case, it is difficult to see what would or should have deflected the board at this point. The basic decision to explore alternative sources of funding seemed wise; no problems surfaced in the consultant's background; her credentials were apparently in order, her fees reasonable; and her plans, to the nonexpert (even to the single expert—the development director) appeared plausible.[39]

The next stage in evaluating compliance by directors with the duty of care is the actual monitoring or follow-up stage. This is one of the most difficult tasks for any board. In the eyes of the law, board conduct tends to be oriented toward action on specific matters or transactions. Monitoring, follow-up, or surveillance is not transactional. In our example, the board received formal reports from the consultant after each of the first two years. In these cases, the consultant offered credible explanations for the disappointing performance. The administrator and development director were closely involved with the progress of the marketing campaign and saw no problem of sufficient magnitude deserving of further inquiry or the board's attention.

At the end of the third year, the board appropriately terminated the arrangement, seeing no upturn in receipts, as had been anticipated at the outset. (It should be noted that the board also might have reasoned otherwise and extended the effort another year or two.) Assuming that the Institute had sufficient financial reserves to mount the campaign in the first place (for example, it didn't have to curtail its operations or jeopardize credit relations with vendors, etc.), it was entirely consistent both with the duty of care and the policy implicit in the business judgment rule to pursue this inherently risky undertaking in light of the Institute's small but growing deficit and the prudent need to explore alternatives.

The judgments by the directors were made in good faith (i.e., at arm's length), informed and plausibly rational. The board's reliance on experts and employees made its deliberations better informed. The delegation of board authority to the development committee to monitor the project's progress, given the size of the Institute's board, was an effective exercise of board power.

Let us suppose, however, that not all members of the development committee nor of the full board are the generalists envisioned by the duty of care. Let us assume that one of the committee members has extensive professional marketing experience as head of his own marketing firm and a second committee member has been the chief volunteer fund-raiser for a major private university with a record of successfully marketing educational services. Are these two directors under any greater burden in demonstrating compliance with the duty of care?

The language of the duty states that it will be adapted to the unique circumstances of each organization and each director. While directors aren't presumed to possess specialized knowledge, if they possess it, they are compelled to use it. In our example, if one of the committee members had greater insight into the proposed marketing plan or had a sound reason to believe it would not succeed, or possessed a professionally informed view of the consultant's qualifications that were not entirely favorable, that director should have alerted the other directors to any reasonably foreseeable problem.

Officers serving as directors and nondirector officers should also use their special skills and knowledge that are relevant to the particular problem. The administrator, whether or not a board member, would be regarded as an officer based on an analysis of his functions and would be subject to a duty to use his extensive knowledge of the Institute's affairs, knowledge much more detailed than that of a volunteer director. Nevertheless, all directors, officers and staff acted in this case within their legal duties and, thus, would not be subject to any liability arising from the failure of the Institute's marketing campaign.

The Business Judgment Rule

The eponymous business judgment rule is a doctrine that has its origins in the conduct of business organizations. The rule provides that judgments by boards about "business" matters are presumptively correct and that businesses function best when those decisions remain inviolable except in cases of egregious misconduct. However, both the precise nature of the rule and the extent to which it applies to non-profit organizations remain uncertain.[40] It is intended to afford directors total protection from liability for business judgments so long as the judgment is plausibly rational, involves no conflicting interest, and the director has acted in a manner that he believes reasonably is informed.[41] The rule is designed to protect honest, informed business judgments in order to allow risk-taking, innovation, and other creative entrepreneurial activities that are at the heart of corporate business enterprise. If a court determines that the business judgment rule applies, it will not undertake an assessment of the more complex and exacting duty of care standard discussed above.

So long as its basic requirements are met, the business judgment rule essentially insulates a board's decision-making process from judicial scrutiny.[42] Neither the business judgment rule nor the duty of care endorse specific outcomes because few complex business decisions are verifiably correct or not correct. They protect a process rather than any specific results. The rationale for doing so in the business context rests on theories about the nature, and optimum functioning, of our fundamental economic arrangements, including their essentially private character.[43]

While the business judgment rule limits inquiry into decisions of business directors, the nonprofit context does not afford the same inherent safeguards of the decision-making process business corporations enjoy. For nonprofit organizations, directors' legal accountability, not market forces, is the principal line of defense against director failure. "[T]here are no shareholders waiting in the wings, assisted by squads of lawyers ready and anxious to commence a derivative action. The stock will not plummet; the organization will not report a decline in earnings or sales—there is no easy way to measure or control the quality of performance."[44]

What, then, is the role of the business judgment rule in the nonprofit context and to what extent should it be applicable to shield erring—but honest—directors from suits over the consequences of their actions? There are few cases which appear to invoke the rule for nonprofits.[45] Two cases involved losses on investments arising out of the Great Depression in which the courts exculpated directors who, however diligent, could not have foreseen the economic havoc wreaked on charitable institutions' investments. To the extent that a version of the business judgment rule insulated directors in these cases, it is unlikely that any different outcome would have resulted were the conduct involved measured by conventional duty of care standards.

A third case appears to have involved a director's conflicting interests and, thus, seems to run counter to most versions of the rule's applicability, which does not protect a director who has a conflict of interest (such a director is not necessarily liable, but is required to comply with the ordinary duty of care). Although these three cases relate to "economic" decisions, its application may extend to other areas of decision making.[46]

Is there a suitable alternative need or justification for the rule for nonprofits and, if so, when should it be applied? To some extent, that justification may be found in the uncompensated nature of the service of the typical nonprofit director, whom courts are reluctant to hold to too exacting a standard of conduct.[47] Also, given the continual struggle of many nonprofits for financial stability, it may be wise for society to encourage a degree of risk-taking in efforts to secure such resources or, alternatively, to effect savings. At the same time, such risk-taking may conflict with the traditional caution of many charitable directors and their perceptions of the importance of preserving capital. The real issue, then, is what best serves the interest of the public as the ultimate beneficiary of the activities of charitable organizations.

On the one hand, we may want to stimulate imaginative and creative use of nonprofit resources, and the business judgment rule would tend to encourage charitable risk-taking.[48] On the other hand, its application to nonprofits might shield from scrutiny important matters of public policy. Both the Revised Model Business Corporation Act (RMBCA) and the Revised Model Nonprofit Corporation Act (RMNCA) leave the content and application of the rule to the courts. While this does not offer definitive guidance, it is doubtful, given the paucity of cases, that the business judgment rule has been or would be determinative in shielding nonprofit directors in any case that involves the duty of care (the rule never shields directors in duty of loyalty situations). Directors still have the clear and considerable protection of the prudent person standard of care, and, when that is properly articulated and applied, opportunity for the business judgment rule would be limited. There seems to be little different between the application by the courts of a "business judgment rule" and the standard of care; directors must act in a grossly negligent fashion in order to be held to have breached their duties.[49] Recent changes in the laws of a number of states limiting director liability, primarily in the duty of care area, further blur any remaining distinction.*

As a consequence primarily of an "insurance" crisis, more than one dozen states have passed measures shielding directors from liability for tort claims and liberalizing indemnification provisions. None of these statutes, however, affect the duty of care directly, but only the consequences of its breach. These changes are discussed in chapter 5, "When Directors Get Sued," and chapter 6, "Protection: Indemnification and Insurance."

Case Studies: the Business Judgment Rule

Risk-Taking Can Be Prudent: A Case for the Business Judgment Rule

In the early 1970s, energy costs rose dramatically, with a particularly adverse affect on nonprofit educational institutions, many of

---

*As a consequence primarily of an "insurance" crisis, more than one dozen states have passed measures shielding directors from liability for tort claims

which were limited in their ability to pass on these costs. The crisis was unusually severe for small Northern liberal arts colleges, already in strained circumstances through endowments eroded by inflation, and long, harsh winters that generated large heating bills.[50]

One such institution, Eliot College, located in a region with abundant natural gas and numerous producing wells, decided it could convert its plant from conventional heating oil to natural gas, thereby achieving considerable savings: almost $400,000 annually, if successful. The idea, originally proffered to Eliot's trustees by a former board member was heartily endorsed by the board. As a first step, the board authorized a preliminary geological survey at the modest cost of $6,500 to determine if Eliot's property was likely to produce. With the receipt of positive test results, but with the knowledge that the odds for success were moderately low, the board then authorized the commencement of a drilling program for which it already had raised $115,000. Two months later, gas was found. Unfortunately, the gas became mixed with water and an additional $20,000 was spent, ultimately without effect, in an attempt to solve the problem.

While Eliot got some usable gas from the well, it would have taken at least four or five more working wells to have met its needs. Meanwhile, fuel costs stabilized in the early 1980s (subsequently declining sharply). As a result, plans to modify the central heating system to accommodate a large gas flow were shelved. Oil still supplies most of the college's energy needs, although at a greatly reduced cost due both to energy conservation programs instituted during the energy crunch as well as the worldwide collapse in oil prices. The board decided, without formally discontinuing the program, not to raise the minimum of $125,000 for a second full-scale exploration effort.

How does the board's action here stack up against the business judgment rule's widely recognized conditions? Was the decision rational? Was it informed? Was it disinterested (vis à vis conflict of interest)? Although the decline of the power of the OPEC cartel and

---

and liberalizing indemnification provisions. None of these statutes, however, affect the duty of care directly, but only the consequences of its breach. These changes are discussed below in chapter 5, "When Directors Get Sued", and chapter 6, "Protection: Indemnification and Insurance."

the reappearance of 80 cent gasoline make the energy shortage of the 1970s a fading memory, the issues it presented, at the height of the crisis were real enough. The events unleashed havoc among small liberal arts colleges, especially in the northern states and even may have contributed to the closing of a few of these institutions.

The search for alternative energy sources was then regarded as a vital exercise, spawning or encouraging, among other things, new and innovative technologies. There can be little doubt that the college's quest for cheap, reliable, alternative energy was rational at the time (by contrast, such a venture today, in the light of the contemporary abundance of energy supplies, might seem a good deal more quixotic).

Then, the college faced mounting utility costs, seemingly without end. The trustees were familiar with the institution's financial condition and with the region's natural resources, including its abundance of natural gas. Committing limited financial resources to pursuing such an endeavor would certainly appear to be a rational choice in the light of the potential rewards: a very significant savings, despite the risk.

The propriety of the trustees' judgment is further buttressed by its being an informed decision. The extent of the information necessary is always measured against the cost of acquiring information. The need for information and the determination of the extent of that need are themselves matters of "business judgment." The board here did not authorize the expenditure of funds for drilling based on a hunch or an uninformed guess. The mere existence of the energy crisis was not itself sufficient to justify any expedient, however outlandish or irrational. What the board did, however, was to authorize, at very limited expense, a survey that then became the basis for an informed decision to proceed, once the positive results of the survey were in hand. The board, of course, could not rule out problems along the way, including those that eventually cropped up. But, it could proceed comfortably, reasonably believing itself to have been informed adequately under the circumstances.

As to the third requisite—that of a disinterested decision-making process—the entire transaction involved no conflicting interests, which would make the safe harbor afforded by the business judgment rule unavailable and relegate the directors, in defending their action, to the more exacting scrutiny imposed under the duty of care.

A second level of analysis would have to be applied to the second major decision, the decision to start the actual drilling program. Each discrete decision calls for the board to exercise informed judgment. With positive test results, the board had to decide whether or not to make the more substantial commitment required for an active exploration and drilling program. The risks involved the expenditure of $100,000 or so while the odds against ultimate success, despite the favorable survey results, remained fairly high. On the other hand, the possible reward, sharply reduced energy costs, was substantial, and the board was successful in raising funds specifically for the project, rather than having to use operating funds. Although there was a good chance that ultimate success might elude the college, the potential rewards were great: significantly reduced energy costs that would remain predictable and stable over the long term.

In any such undertaking—as in many commercial ventures— often the hardest decision is knowing when persistence involves "throwing good money after bad." The protection of the business judgment rule applies not just to affirmative decisions— commissioning a survey, authorizing the exploration, committing additional funds to devise a means for separating gas from water—but to decisions not to fund additional wells even when a formal decision is not taken. Here, given the partial success of the first attempt, the lack of funds for further efforts (which might be worth pursuing if stimulated by a completely successful first effort), and the resulting need to tap other sources for the extra financing, the board's decision not to continue the program was well-supported.

It should be clear, however, how highly circumstantial all such decisions are. With the modification of only a few key facts, the board's unobjectionable conduct could become irresponsible. If, for example, a board member with considerable local real-estate holdings, who had already done some wildcatting on his property, had proposed the initial venture, the board's decision might have been different. Increased knowledge about the geological conditions on Eliot College land certainly would be of substantial value to a trustee owning adjacent land, especially one with an active drilling program.

Although not a conflicting interest within the strict confines of the typical conflicts statute—requiring the trustee's abstention in voting on a drilling plan—such an interest would probably be sufficient to preclude the application of the business judgment rule. In such a situation, the board's action, however, might still be seen as having complied with the duty of care, but there would be a more searching examination of the board's decision under full duty of care norms.

Similarly, if drilling a single well cost $250,000 and six were needed to supply a substantial portion of the college's needs, the entire enterprise would be a much more risky way (an immediate expenditure of $1,500,000 if all were successful) of trying to save $400,000 per year. A change in the number of wells needed, the cost per well, the odds of a dry or otherwise problematic hole, the projected savings and the extent of competing demands for limited funds—any of these factors could make an otherwise rational and, therefore, supportable decision not rational and, hence, insupportable.

What Is Enough Information?: The Business Judgment Rule and Decision Making

Good Haven is a nonprofit corporation that operates a number of programs for the homeless, including housing facilities with social service programs. Good Haven was active on behalf of the homeless long before it became fashionable. Much of its work is carried out in the skid row section of Mahagonny, a Midwestern city whose downtown was virtually abandoned in the 1950s and 1960s. Good Haven owns and rents numerous properties scattered throughout the downtown area, including some surrounding the city's once grand but now virtually abandoned railroad station. These buildings house Good Haven's offices and all of its programs, including the shelters. Its large board is typical of a publicly supported charity in a mid-sized city: business and professional people and a smattering of clergy, academics and social workers, with a couple of respectable "activists."

During the last several years, Mahagonny has started to "come back." It is currently in the midst of a minor boom and real estate values are increasing after years of stagnation. The centerpiece of

Mahagonny's resurgence is the almost completed renovation of the old railroad station, helped by a massive infusion of public funds.

Good Haven has been given the chance to purchase a large commercial office building within walking distance of the station. Located on a full block front, the building is still fully tenanted, although at rather modest rentals, with a mix of commercial and professional occupants. Purchase of this building will enable Good Haven to consolidate most of its programs, now dispersed at sites throughout downtown Mahagonny. In addition, a number of board members see an opportunity for Good Haven to share in the booming real estate market fueled by the station's redevelopment.

The sales price for the building is $5.8 million, and renovation will come to $1.9 million, which Good Haven will pay be assuming an existing $2.5 million mortgage and by borrowing an additional $5.2 million from a local bank, secured by a mortgage on its existing real estate, including a second mortgage on the office building. The proceeds of the borrowing will enable Good Haven to undertake substantial renovation to upgrade the attractiveness of the facility and cover all closing costs.

The annual expense for servicing the two mortgages comes to approximately $1.2 million. Good Haven will save approximately $400,000 by consolidating its existing rental facilities in the new building, which can be expected to produce $450,000 per year in rental income. This leaves Good Haven with an annual shortfall of $350,000.

Good Haven in the past has sought no government funding and has been supported almost entirely by private contributions. The board believes that it can close any projected deficit by increasing rental charges in the newly acquired building and by raising additional private contributions. No exhaustive investigation, however, has been made of these alternatives because of the pressure to accept or reject the offer on the building and close the deal within a period of three weeks.

If the board authorizes the transaction, is it protected by the business judgment rule? If not, are the directors, in authorizing the deal, nevertheless protected from liability because they complied with their duty of care?

The salient feature presented by these facts is the need to make critical decisions within a compressed schedule and on the basis of incomplete information. We are not dealing here either with an interested director or an irrational decision. The main issue under the business judgment rule is whether or not the board possessed sufficient information to justify its decision. An irrational decision—one not based on adequate information—is not shielded by the rule. The directors must believe that they are informed about the decision to be made, and there must be some objective support for that belief.[51]

The business judgment rule permits directors to take into account the severe time pressure under which real decisions must frequently be made and the limitations thus imposed. These time limitations may compel a degree of risk-taking, including the possibility of not being in possession of all of the relevant facts. A decision to accept the risk of incomplete information would be permitted when the directors reasonably believe such informational risk-taking is justified.

There cannot be any way to quantify how much information will establish the required "reasonable belief." Among the factors used in judging a director's reasonable belief of what was appropriate are: (1) How important is the judgment the board faces? (2) How much time is available for obtaining more information? (3) How much will it cost to obtain the information? (Will lawyers, accountants, appraisers, etc., have to be hired to evaluate the information?) (4) If a board committee or staff or outside experts have explored a particular matter and presented their views to the board, how much confidence does the board put in them? and (5) What is the general condition of the organization at the time, including the competing demands for board attention?

The personal business or professional experience of a director or officer may help to inform him about a decision. He may also be informed by the general views or specialized experience of colleagues. Reliance on reports of the officers and staff of the organization or on outside professionals often will be necessary and, in many situations, will satisfy the informational requirements. Business judgments often are made on the basis of imperfect information, and a director's judgment as to how much information was needed should not be unfairly second-guessed.[52] The important decision confronting the Good Haven directors demonstrates the pervasive need to make judgments with only imperfect information available, and the inherent risks involved.

The Good Haven directors have been offered an unusual opportunity that can confer substantial benefits on the organization: greatly enhanced program capacity and potentially substantial economic rewards. The element of risk involves the inability, due to the time pressures, to assess whether the rental market for the building can sustain additional increases sufficient to offset the projected deficit, and whether the organization's fund-raising efforts can be extended to realize a comparable increase. To review either the rental market or Good Haven's fund-raising capacity in any meaningful way would take too much time. An additional factor militating in favor of the proposal would be the expected reluctance of the bank financing the purchase to foreclose on Good Haven properties in the event of a default and the likelihood that it would encourage a "work-out" of any loan default, with the least disruptive effect on the organization.*

Given the diversity of the Good Haven board and the varied skills and backgrounds of its members, as well as its own extensive and successful experience with fund-raising, the presentation of the proposal at a meeting in which questions were asked and a variety of views considered could address the informational gaps. In such a case, the board, if it approved the proposed transaction, would be making an informed, rational decision and would be acting well within the confines of the business judgment rule.

It is important to understand, however, that business judgments are never or almost never verifiably correct or incorrect. The rule protects a process rather than a result because the nature of that process is considered to afford superior results overall. In any specific application, the rule dictates no particular outcome. The Good Haven directors might just as easily have concluded that Good Haven should

---

*Good Haven might reduce the inherent risks in the transaction by forming a wholly-owned subsidiary to purchase and own the property. Assuming Good Haven properly maintains the subsidiary's separate existence, such an approach might minimize the consequence of a potential default (although such a strategy could have less effect if, as might be expected, the bank sought Good Haven's guarantee of its subsidiary's obligations).

not pursue the transaction because of the projected deficit and the uncertainty that enhanced rentals might be forthcoming and that intensified fund-raising initiatives would be successful. That decision as well would be protected by an application of the business judgment rule.

The Duty of Loyalty

The Nature of the Duty

We live in an economic system devoted to private gain and the individual rewards and broader social benefits that are believed to flow from maximizing opportunities for such gain. In enshrining a duty of loyalty, the law recognizes the power of these financial incentives, i.e., it acknowledges that the ability to consider the best interests of an institution in a careful, rational, and evenhanded manner may be clouded by the temptation of personal financial benefit. All of the prescriptions for director conduct (and the discussions of care and skill and diligence) are premised on an undivided loyalty that, alone, can assure the necessary disinterest while considering an organization's business. Thus, when questions of loyalty arise, director conduct will be more intensely scrutinized than when issues of care alone are presented, and the liberalized standard of the business judgment rule, would not be available to directors whose conduct is challenged about a conflict of interest even if other issues also are involved.[53]

The basic duty of loyalty, which is similar for nonprofits and business corporations, requires a director to have an undivided allegiance to the organization's mission (see the discussion of the duty of obedience, below) when using either the power of his position or information he possesses concerning the organization or its property. And it bars a director from using his position or information concerning the organization and its property in a manner that allows him to secure a pecuniary benefit for himself.[54] This duty also may be violated by pursuing the financial interest of a third person[55] (even if that third person is another charitable organization).[56] While the proper disclosure of the existence and nature of such a conflict and the

59

authorization of the transaction by a disinterested decision maker acting for the organization can relax these constraints, the director's conduct, at all times, must further the organization's goals and not his
own interests.

Breaches of the duty of loyalty in a nonprofit context involve
more than simple misconduct by directors; when an organization is
permitted to become a vehicle for private gain, such breaches are a
subversion of the nonprofit nature of the organization itself. The pro-
scription of private gain invariably imposed on charities by the Internal Revenue Service,[57] generally by state law (which restricts purposes
and bars personal financial gain),[58] and typically by the governing
instruments of an organization (which incorporate Internal Revenue
Code and state law requirements) all reflect the encompassing nature
of the duty of loyalty.

The Statutory Formulations

Unlike the duty of care, there is no comprehensive formulation
of the duty of loyalty.[59] A number of state nonprofit laws do deal with
two significant manifestations of duty of loyalty problems: transactions in which directors have conflicts of interest and—although more
widespread, of less significance—loans to directors (only nineteen
states have general conflict provisions, while forty-seven proscribe
some loans to officers and directors).[60] Nonprofit laws also generally
prohibit the distribution of any earnings or profits to directors. This
nondistribution constraint, however, is so extensive that it is more
accurately viewed as a defining characteristic of nonprofits rather than
a species of self dealing. Because of that, and its noncontroversial
character, it is not discussed here.

The conflict of interests statutes cover only particular types of
financial conflicts of interests. At one time, contracts between corporations (whether nonprofit or business) and their directors were prohibited. With the increasing prominence of the corporation,
prohibiting such contracts became increasingly impractical. As a consequence, those laws were modified and such contracts made voidable
only in limited circumstances. If the director with the conflict lived up

to his duty of loyalty by dealing fairly with the corporation, the contract would be allowed.[61]

Existing nonprofit statutes all share pretty much the same history as their business corporate counterparts, although the trust-law legacy of nonprofits may make the application of the duty of loyalty somewhat more inflexible in the nonprofit context. Courts, in those states without a specific statute, that have considered these loyalty issues reach generally similar results.[62]

The duty of loyalty, however, is far broader than conflict of interests transactions. Conflict statutes simply deal with one aspect of that duty they specify under what circumstances a self-dealing transaction may be attacked and of what procedures a director with a conflict of interest may avail himself to sustain an otherwise voidable transaction. These statutes, however, may not completely insulate conflicts of interests either from judicial scrutiny of their inherent fairness or from attack on a basis unconnected to the duty of loyalty (if, for example, noninterested directors negligently approve a conflicts transaction, thereby violating their duty of care).[63]

Conflicts tend to be narrowly defined: the personal financial interest of a director must be involved. Such interests would include the financial interests of a spouse, a dependent family member, and, perhaps, other family members or close associates. They also include indirect financial interests through corporations and partnerships. They generally exclude important nonfinancial conflicts (which may be particularly important for nonprofits, where directors often sit on multiple boards, including those of grantmakers and grantseekers).[64]

Depending on the statute, the disclosure required of a director seeking approval for a conflict of interests transaction will cover the material facts of the conflicting interests themselves (for example, the extent of a director's interest in a supplier of goods to the nonprofit organization on whose board he sits) as well as the specific terms of the proposed contract or other transaction between the nonprofit organization and the conflicting entity. The full board or committee (or other appropriate body)[65] reviewing the contract or transaction must approve it by a disinterested majority,[66] although interested directors may generally be counted toward a quorum and may cast a nondecisive vote.

In approving any such transaction, the other noninterested directors must exercise their normal "business judgment" or "duty of care" vigilance and so must believe rationally that the transaction is a proper one for the organization, despite its manifest benefits to their fellow director.[67] A transaction of perceived unfairness would not qualify; the noninterested directors' approval would not comport with their duty of care or the requirements of the business judgment rule. When such disinterested approval is unattainable, the transaction or contract will still be immune from successful attack if it is subsequently demonstrated to a court to be fair. However, in such a situation, the interested director bears the burden of establishing fairness.

These statutes provide substantially more favorable treatment to conflict of interests transactions where approval has been sought in advance, rather than after the fact. Advance approval allows an organization to seek to negotiate more favorable terms, if appropriate, and it encourages the disclosure of conflicting interests. When that is not done, a director attempting to sustain a challenged transaction must affirmatively establish its fairness.

An important factor in evaluating the fairness of a transaction is whether or not the organization has been independently represented in negotiating the terms of the transaction by an individual without any conflicting interest. Fairness also is supported when the transaction has not been initiated by the director with the conflicting interest, but by some other director or officer or an unrelated party. Although the extent of a director's potential profit from a conflict transaction that is "fair" to the organization need not always be disclosed (only his "interest" in the other party to the transaction—for example, that he owns 14 percent of the stock of a supplier), the profitability of a particular transaction at issue to the interested director would be a factor in assessing fairness.[68]

Courts' View of Loyalty Transgressions

Because many states lack statutory treatments of conflict of interests transactions and their treatment is only one facet of the many-sided duty of loyalty in states that do have such laws, the courts have been important in defining the full reach of that duty. Court decisions on conflicting interests tend to require more extensive disclosure than the statutes dealing with the same subject, even, at times, superimposing a standard of fairness, regardless of the adequacy of disclosure and the procedure for approval. For example, they require "full disclosure and fair dealing"[69] or "full disclosure" and "full value"[70] or some similar formula,[71] and the courts have not hesitated to unwind transactions when the indicia of fairness are lacking, even if some disclosure has been made.[72]

Most of the cases that deal with loyalty issues involve either the use of corporate property for personal ends, generally with consequent financial loss to the organization, or the appropriation for personal gain of an opportunity suitable for acquisition by the organization (a "corporate opportunity"). Examples of the former typically involve property transactions with directors[73] and the investment or use of corporate assets to promote the personal businesses of directors[74] (or a related third party).[75] The latter arise when an opportunity presents itself—such as the purchase of real estate or of a business that would further the organization's goals—and a director or officer takes advantage of his position to appropriate that opportunity for himself, usually by virtue of superior access or information, thereby depriving the organization he is supposed to serve of a valuable benefit.[76]

In very few of the cases involving self-dealing transactions of the type that would be covered by the typical conflict of interests statute or the appropriation of a corporate opportunity have the courts upheld the challenged conduct. Thus, whether the courts employ the language of trust law, which absolutely bars self-dealing, or the more flexible corporate standard, the results are virtually the same. The exception involves those instances in which the alleged self-dealing challenges internal organizational arrangements for compensation of employed officers who, arguably, exercise control.[77] While fixing the compensation of directors and officers is clearly a form of self-dealing, virtually all nonprofit and corporate statutes today explicitly permit this. Some statutes, like New York's, however, impose a requirement that any such compensation arrangements be reasonable, a requirement the IRS would impose to assure that an exempt organization was not distributing earnings or profits to officers under the guise of compensation.

The only apparent difference between courts applying trust-influenced principles and those applying corporate ones is the nature of the remedy. In most of the decided cases, the self-dealing director is required to restore the opportunity appropriated or the benefit received, but is not otherwise penalized. However, the application of a strict trust standard would require the return of any profits to the organization and require that any property so diverted be held for the organization's benefit (a so-called "constructive trust"). Yet even those courts that speak in harsher terms and impose stricter penalties do little more than restore the status quo.[78]

How to Avoid and Manage Conflicts of Interests

There are basic measures that can be implemented to minimize conflict of interests. Among other things, the composition of the board can be quite important. Conflict-of-interests problems certainly are more likely with a weak board dominated by one or a small group of individuals who, as full-time officers and/or employees, have a financial interest in the organization (even if limited to their salaries and related benefits). The board should consist predominantly of individuals who are financially disinterested. If it is important to have chief executive and/or operating officers on the board, then there must be a weighty counterforce (i.e., independent, unaffiliated directors), since a skillful chief executive officer, in the long run, can easily dominate a part-time volunteer board. One way to achieve the right mix is to exclude any "inside" or otherwise interested directors from the nominating process and provide "independent" directors with sufficient continuity (for example, through boards elected with staggered terms). Such an arrangement would enable the independent directors to accumulate a reservoir of knowledge and experience that would offset the greater familiarity and access of the insiders.

Nevertheless, actual and potential conflicts are likely for most organizations (and are not always the product of an undesirable situation).[79] It is essential that organizations adopt policies to deal with conflicts or they will have to rely on the law, which sets only minimum standards or an *ad hoc* approach, which tends to personalize decisions and either inhibit a frank exchange of views among board members or alienate them. While a formal conflict of interests standard need not be adopted so long as a sufficiently clear way to handle conflicts is understood by the board, a formal policy is almost always preferable to avoid "misunderstandings."

There are any number of sources for developing such a policy, and it is best left to legal counsel to elaborate on the specifics. There are some elements that all policies should address. Foremost among them is a form of disclosure by directors and officers to elicit appropriate information (financial and otherwise, including significant non-profit affiliations). This should be done in the least intrusive way possible and with the greatest sensitivity for the personal privacy of those affected (whether through the formality of a questionnaire or otherwise), if it is to be effective and supported by the board.

Conflicts of interests should be viewed as extraordinary occurrences when they do arise and, therefore, should be handled with circumspection.[80] In many cases, this will mean adopting procedures and taking measures that go beyond the law's strictures.[81] Thus, while the law both allows an interested director's voting on a transaction that involves a conflict and does not preclude his participating in discussion and debate, there seems to be little good reason for allowing this participation. Either the conflicted director's participation is unnecessary for review and approval of the transaction, in which case it is, at best, superfluous, or it is essential for approval or at least persuasion, in which case that is exactly the consequence that the law seeks to proscribe. In any case, an organization should receive only disinterested representation in negotiating the terms of and implementing an interested transaction.[82]

Although many statutes do not require an organization to establish affirmatively the fairness of such transactions, particularly where there has been disclosure and disinterested advance approval, efforts to do so should always be made. California law, for example, requires a finding by the board that a more advantageous arrangement could not have been obtained with reasonable effort under the circumstances.[83] This can be particularly important in those situations in which all directors (or all but one) have an interest in the transaction making disinterested approval impossible.

It is important, in conserving public good will and in avoiding embarrassing public scrutiny, to be able to establish fairness. It also may insulate the noninterested directors from attack if they approve a transaction of known unfairness. Again, this doesn't mean that elaborate procedures need be adopted. Much depends on the nature of the proposed transaction and the size and complexity of the organization. Procedures can range from formal, competitive bidding on major contracts to comparison shopping by obtaining informal price quotations for simple goods and services. The key is that there be a reasonable effort to ascertain the fairness of any such transaction.

Special mention must be made about private foundations. The Internal Revenue Code superimposes on these grant-making institutions a set of special rules, which apply to transactions that the Code characterizes as "self-dealing" transactions. These prohibitions include only those matters recognized by state law as involving conflicts, but also cover both individuals and transactions that would not be subject to challenge under state law. Violation of the self-dealing rules may lead to financial penalties on the self-dealing individuals and, if not corrected, on the foundation itself, and can even lead to the loss of tax exemption.[84] These regulations are highly technical and foundation officers and directors, with the assistance of legal counsel, should familiarize themselves generally with this complex area and should not approach any potential self-dealing transaction without legal advice.

There is an additional cautionary note that should be struck here. An entirely different set of loyalty-conflicts problems are being created as nonprofits in the 1980s have moved increasingly into the commercial arena.[85] In this, as in other areas of the law, new rules may have to be developed for situations simply not dreamt of when existing laws dealing with conflicts were developed and refined.[86]

Increasingly complex transactions involving multi-tiered corporate structures, joint ventures with profit-oriented corporations or partnerships, affiliated or subsidiary business corporations and the like, raise a number of troubling legal issues not only for the organizations themselves, but also for directors. For example, to whom is a duty of loyalty owed when a nonprofit director serves on the board of a business corporation subsidiary or joint venture partner at the request of the nonprofit?[87] How are the ultimately differing objectives of nonprofit and for-profit partners to be resolved, and what about the director who serves both? Reconciling the competing tensions may be difficult; how do you isolate, in a related organization, activities more likely to generate liabilities without completely surrendering control? How do you continue to influence related organizations without causing them to delegate decision-making authority improperly or without ignoring corporate formalities intended to confer protection on risk-prone undertakings?[88]

Unfortunately, there is little precedent in this area to guide the director and no certain answers or even clear principles to follow. While a thoughtful definition of the objectives to be attained in any such endeavor, careful documentation, full and frank disclosure of all conflicting interests, and liberal indemnification provisions may minimize the problems, these developments could still open up whole new areas of liability. For that reason, directors should be aware that the concern with conflicts of interests is not a static one and will be shaped by the important forces shaping nonprofit activities generally.

Loans to Directors

The one specific area that a number of nonprofit statutes address is the ban on loans to officers and directors.[89] Although a majority of states (thirty) flatly ban such transactions, there are certain exceptions such as California, which permits mortgage loans to finance the purchase of a principal residence for officers and directors.[90] New York's education law, limited to educational nonprofits (primarily colleges and universities), has provisions similar to the California law.[91] Because nonprofit compensation levels tend to be quite modest, housing-related loans or financing programs can often be important if organizations are to attract and retain competent staff and officers. In effect, such loans simply may be viewed as a form of "reasonable compensation."

A small number of states, however, permit such loans if they confer some benefit on the nonprofit corporation or otherwise further some legitimate corporate objective. Apart from such special needs (as financing housing, moving expenses, and the like), any such transaction (especially if the beneficiary is a volunteer director and not an employed officer) is likely to cause scrutiny by regulatory authorities or raise public concern and would best be avoided.[92] It must be emphasized that this prohibition does not preclude loans or advances to employees of nonprofits either individually or in the implementation of some general policy, nor does it limit the opportunities for compensating staff (and directors) in an appropriate fashion.

Case Studies: the Duty of Loyalty

Where's Mine?: Appropriating a Corporate Opportunity

Camp Uplift, owned by the Camp Uplift Association, Inc., a nonprofit corporation, is a long-established New England summer camp, located on 112 acres in one of the most beautiful areas of southern Vermont. The camp has a substantial endowment and has used this to provide scholarship assistance to inner-city children and to assure itself of the best counselors, instructors, and supervisors representing diverse origins, education, and skills.

For a time in the 1960s and 1970s, summer camps experienced a period of relative unpopularity. Coupled with a declining youth population, the camp incurred operating losses for several years. For a number of summers, the scope of Uplift's activities had to be curtailed. Enrollments were reduced modestly and scholarship assistance was cut back.

In 1978, the board reviewed the possibility of closing the camp and selling the land for development as seasonal homes (the area in which the camp is located is prime vacation territory). A sale of the camp would bring substantial financial rewards, which then could be used to fund other activities consistent with the association's purposes as set forth in its governing instruments. No formal board action was ever taken on a possible sale of the camp property and, as the 1980s began, there was a resurgence of interest in summer camps. With the "Baby Boomers" own belated baby boom, Uplift's prospects—long- and short-term—were completely restored.

In 1979, Abel Glance, the camp's executive director for the last twenty-two years, purchased from a neighbor of the camp who had no involvement with it, a sixty-acre parcel of land adjacent to the camp's main property. Mr. Glance made no disclosure of this transaction, either to the board or any other officer of the association. Although many years ago the camp had considered expansion, such plans had been abandoned for some time. After the boom years of the early 1980s, however, the board is once again considering expansion. Such plans contemplate the purchase of adjoining land for development on a joint venture basis with a commercial developer, both to realize income and to preserve the character of the countryside from unwelcome and chaotic growth. Through a local real estate broker, Mr. Glance now offers the property to the camp, at a hefty profit for himself. What position should the board take and what legal exposure, if any, does Mr. Glance have?

The corporate opportunity doctrine is a variant of the director's duty of loyalty, and, in general, there is no difference in the way in which such corporate opportunity transactions are scrutinized by the courts from those involving direct conflicts of interests that are typically dealt with by statute. A director or officer is permitted to deal with his organization so long as he deals fairly with full disclosure of relevant facts, and, unless the organization is independently represented by disinterested directors in passing on such a transaction, the director with the divided interest bears the burden of proving the fairness of any proposed dealing with the corporation.

A full-time officer, like Mr. Glance (here, the chief full-time officer), could reasonably be expected to be aware of the camp's historic, although momentarily quiescent interest, in expansion of its physical facilities and its legitimate interest in protecting its environs from incompatible land uses. In contrast, a nonofficer director, with service on the board of limited duration, might not appreciate the full significance of the camp's interest in the property.

69

If Mr. Glance were challenged on his proposed sale to the camp, as he should be, he could be required to sell the property to the camp, at his cost, or, in an ensuing legal action, he could be compelled to hold the property in constructive trust for the camp. The association then would be entitled to buy it from him at his purchase price (without reflecting any increase in fair market value nor the value of any improvements he made to it). Additionally, the executive director would be obligated to turn over to the camp any profit realized during the period of his ownership (for example, rental income that he may have derived from it in the interim, etc.).

As with most duty of loyalty issues, there are few absolutes. A director or officer may take advantage of a corporate opportunity if he has presented it to an independent decision-making body. The board here would be independent. When doing so, he would have to make full disclosure of both the relevant facts surrounding the conflicting interests and the nature of the corporate opportunity (if not already known to the board); finally, if the organization declines to take advantage of the proffered opportunity, it must do so on a rational basis (for example, because it lacks the financial resources to acquire or exploit it, or is legally restricted from accepting it, or is otherwise not interested in it for a legitimate reason related exclusively to its own goals).

Again, as with most loyalty issues, the rules concerning a corporate opportunity are broadly protective in nature to assure that an organization is dealt with fairly by its directors and officers. Yet, they are not so rigid as to preclude any dealing with the organization, and they reflect an appropriate distinction between full-time officers, whose activities are more circumscribed, and volunteer directors, who are given greater latitude.

The Charismatic Executive: Using Corporate Property

Dr. Carker is the formidable executive director of Salamander, an organization he founded ten years ago. Salamander is devoted to enhancing public awareness of the problem of teenage suicide and employs intensive counseling and other therapeutic strategies to develop an effective treatment program.

The organization receives its funding from a mix of government grants, foundation and corporate contributions, and public solicitations. It is governed by a fifteen-person board of directors (including Dr. Carker). Many of the directors are celebrities or wealthy supporters of the program who have been attracted by the forcefulness of Dr. Carker's personality and by a shared concern over the suicide problem. Others are successful professionals and business people with similar motivations. Dr. Carker is regarded by the board members as a unique and charismatic personality who has dealt effectively with a singular personal tragedy.

In the organization's formative years, Dr. Carker himself developed many of the therapeutic approaches used by Salamander and supervised much of the actual treatment. Recently, he has abandoned many of these managerial and supervisory responsibilities. His attention has turned increasingly to other concerns: proselytizing on behalf of the organization's program and other, unrelated issues, which he sees as part of a complex of social problems clouding the nation's future.

In the last 2 years, of the 235-or-so working days each year, Dr. Carker has spent 165 days and 198 days, respectively, traveling and speaking, largely about his broad social agenda. Less than one-quarter of that time has been spent in situations that confer any direct benefit on Salamander's program.

In the early days of the organization, staff, including Dr. Carker, shared in the material privations common to fledgling voluntary organizations with a strong sense of mission. With success, however, has come an imperial style. Travel and accommodation are always first-class; entertaining is lavish and expensive; and Dr. Carker is almost invariably accompanied by a retinue of Salamander employees as personal aides. Although Dr. Carker's direct compensation of $150,000 is high—but acceptable for a professional of his experience, skill, and attainments—the value of his travel and entertainment expenses brings the total cost of supporting his activities to almost $400,000 (approximately 5 percent of the organization's total budget).

This situation has created some concern among officers and fellow board members. Most recently, one of Salamander's fiscal officers was dismissed when he questioned the business purpose of an expense voucher submitted by one of the doctor's aides following a recent trip. The seriousness of the matter was reflected in a preliminary inquiry made by the state attorney general. Any ensuing scandal would be highly injurious to Salamander's programmatic efforts, which are finally beginning to bear fruit. Has Dr. Carker violated any of his duties to Salamander, and, if so, what should the board do?

One of the clearest instances of self-dealing between directors and the organizations that they serve is compensation. Obviously, the payment of compensation to a director, whether required by contract or otherwise, is a form of self-dealing. Yet payments for services, including service as a director or officer, is such an inherent aspect of corporate affairs that some statutes that deal with conflicts of interests make specific exceptions to establish a board's unqualified power to fix the compensation of directors. This is important when dealing with nonemployee directors, whose compensation, in the absence of such exceptions, might be subject to challenge because of the lack of a disinterested decision maker to approve such payments (since all directors, presumably, receive the same fees and would be equally "interested" by virtue of such payments).

Even meeting the rigors of the typical conflicts statute should not be burdensome when dealing with direct compensation. In most cases, the board will possess all the necessary information concerning the "conflict" and the director's or officer's interest (i.e., their compensation) and, thus, no disclosure problem generally arises. This is one situation in which the conflicted director or officer is in possession of no greater information than the entire board (in assessing fairness, the board could rely on any study of comparable salaries prepared by experts or with care by the staff).

More difficult issues arise with "indirect" compensation. When travel and entertainment expenses for directors and officers appear to exceed what is reasonable or customary, they generate a number of potentially troubling legal issues, including private gain, negligence and waste, the duty of obedience, etc. Here, the key is the duty of loyalty of Salamander's chief executive and guiding force. That duty, which enjoins directors and senior officers to pursue the organization's interest to the exclusion, if necessary, of their own personal interests (and those of others), is violated when personal financial benefits or the private agenda of a director or officer become the motivating force behind particular actions.

As the executive director has turned his attention to other interests, the overriding duty to pursue the organization's objectives has been compromised. In that regard, the executive director may be breaching the duty of obedience. In pursuing those objectives in a way that directly subsidizes an increasingly extravagant life-style, the executive director is breaching his duty of loyalty as well, by ignoring the organization's interests in conserving travel funds. The use of Salamander staff for meeting his personal needs also violates that same duty. Employees have duties to perform only in furtherance of the organization's goals, and the diversion of their efforts to satisfy the personal preferences of an executive director visibly manifest a disregard of the organization's welfare and interests. In both cases—the lavish expenditures at organizational expense for personal gratification and the use of corporate personnel—charitable resources are being appropriated for personal ends and the duty of loyalty is being violated.

The best response to such a problem, if personal liability is to be avoided, is the adoption and enforcement of adequate internal financial controls that cover policies governing the use of corporate resources, including the regulation of travel and entertainment expenses. Such policies can be flexible; there may be appropriate occasions for permitting or encouraging more substantial expenditures. But when personal preference and inclination become mixed with the pursuit of organizational goals, serious problems can arise.

This situation is not like the typical conflict of interests transaction. The use of some corporate resources is a necessary part of compensating executives for their services. Arguably, the errant executive director may be pursuing the organization's interests generally, and his own only to the extent of "doing well by doing good."

In such a situation, to forestall possible liability on the part of the executive director for his breach of the duty of loyalty to the organization or by the other directors for breach of their duty of care in permitting such conduct to go unchecked, a protective approach is the most effective.[93] By addressing the problem before it occurs, the directors would have their best opportunity of avoiding any personal liability, at least on the part of the other directors. Otherwise, the continued breach by the executive director of his duty of loyalty by using corporate resources for his own personal needs would lead to his personal liability, with the likelihood of his having to reimburse the organization for benefits he received improperly. The board, once it became aware of the situation, is obligated by the duty of care to act, and its failure to do so could lead ultimately to liability for the individual board members. Duty of loyalty violations generally preclude the protection offered directors by indemnification and D&O insurance.*

Making Friends and Influencing People: Use of Corporate Position

Arthur Megabucks is a long-time trustee of Vespucci University, the dominant institution of higher education in the City of New Hustle. Mr. Megabucks, since graduating from his alma mater forty-five years earlier, has amassed one of the great American fortunes. His personal lifetime charitable contributions have amounted to more than $25 million, including more than $6 million to VU over the years, and he chairs the development committee of the University's board of trustees. From time to time, Mr. Megabucks has discussed with VU's senior development officer the possibility of a major share for the university in his estate (this could amount to at least $100 million).

VU is one of the largest landholders in New Hustle. Since the late 1950s, the area surrounding the main VU campus has deteriorated markedly. To help keep its outstanding academic reputation and to continue to attract an elite student body and leading scholars, VU,

---

*How directors become liable when a duty is breached is discussed at length in chapter 5, and indemnification and insurance are discussed in chapter 6.

with the occasional help of federal, state, and local government agencies as well as private funders, has maintained almost singlehandedly some reasonable quality of life in its environs.

Over the years, VU has focused much of its efforts on preserving the neighborhood's housing stock by rehabilitating many abandoned and deteriorating buildings, frequently working with community groups. VU regards itself as predominantly an urban university and views its relations with its diverse neighbors as a significant aspect of the educational mission it fulfills.

By dint of these efforts, the neighborhood surrounding VU finally is experiencing something of a renaissance. Although there have been no major commercial incursions into this relatively placid environment, the Metropolitan Colossus Association (MCA), the corporation of which Arthur Megabucks is the CEO and largest single shareholder, has started making discreet inquiries of local realtors and small property owners. MCA has very substantial real estate interests throughout New Hustle, including neighborhoods near the VU campus.

For some time VU and a local development group have been involved in acquiring a site for construction of ninety-four units of low- and moderate-income housing, with mixed retail space and community amenities. VU has an informal understanding with the local development group about its commitment to funding and completing the project. The project site abuts the main VU campus and has attractive, unobstructed views of its verdant grounds. MCA has coveted this site for some time and believes it can undertake successfully the first commercial redevelopment in the VU area in many years. Megabucks has repeatedly indicated his displeasure with VU's apparent intention to proceed with its commitment to the local development corporation.

During several private meetings with the director of development, several fellow trustees and the university's president, Megabucks has made it clear that he intends to make a major testamentary gift to VU. In the course of these meetings, he has articulated his own vision of the campus, which includes a pivotal role for MCA in redeveloping the area. This, he noted, would have extremely favorable financial consequences for VU's existing real estate holdings. He has urged the university to pull back from its neighborhood preservation activities and cede its development role to the private sector.

Under pressure from MCA and Megabucks, VU has let its long-pending plans for the ninety-four units of housing flounder, and they now seem unlikely to take place. Instead, the president has proposed that the trustees authorize a "master plan" for the development of the surrounding area with a view toward recruiting significant private-sector participation. No mention has been made of any private discussions with Megabucks. The rationale for this change in direction is the obvious financial incentive for VU and the continuing need for the area's redevelopment. The trustees approve the development of the master plan, and, ultimately, MCA becomes a major participant in the redevelopment program with highly profitable financial results.

This situation involves possible violations of the duty of loyalty by Mr. Megabucks, the director of development (as an officer of the institution), VU's president and those fellow trustees who were aware of the potentially conflicting interests of trustee Megabucks. Because duty of loyalty problems are a common occurrence, there is no over-riding policy that all transactions involving conflicts should be avoided at all costs and under all circumstances. The prevailing laws dealing with conflicts are intended to encourage disclosure and fair dealing. Here, there has been no disclosure of the potential interest that Megabucks and MCA have in altering a well-established corporate policy (VU's long-standing community redevelopment activities) and in securing the trustees' approval for the master plan.

By failing to disclose his interests, Megabucks may not take advantage either of the "safe harbor" statutes, which permit conflicts of interests transactions when there has been full disclosure and disinterested approval, or their common law counterparts. Disclosure to individual officers and a few fellow board members (i.e., the director of development, the president, and a handful of sympathetic trustees) is not a substitute for disclosure to the board because directors act only in their collective capacity.

Megabucks lacks the undivided loyalty expected of directors. A director may not use his position or information concerning an organization to secure for himself (or a third person) a financial benefit, which is not properly authorized by the governing board on a fully informed basis.[94] Megabucks has exploited his dominant position as trustee, chair of the development committee, and major philanthropist to gain a change in VU's commitment to low income housing, not because the new master plan is a better policy for VU, but because it furthers the financial interest of a company he dominates (MCA). He has misused information to which he is privy by virtue of his position as trustee solely to enhance his personal position. This misuse of corporate position and information by Megabucks for his own benefit violates his duty of loyalty to VU, whether or not his action causes it harm. Any MCA development contracts arising from the breach of Megabucks' duty might be unenforceable against VU (if it so chose), and Megabucks and MCA could be subject to monetary damages (if financial injury to VU could be shown to have occurred) or equitable relief, including, cancellation of the contracts or restitution.[95]

The more difficult issue for nonprofits is a misuse of position or information or property (i.e., Megabucks' misuse of his power) when there is no element of personal benefit, arguably the case here. Such judgments are difficult to make: nonprofit objectives are diffuse, difficult to quantify, and susceptible to different interpretations. It is easier to ascertain the extent of the benefit to the self-dealer as a measure of wrongdoing. Here, for example, while Megabucks has redirected VU housing policy, it would be difficult to say that such policy was the university's "mission" or objective, the latter presumably being higher education, or that the university was clearly harmed by abandoning its neighborhood preservation strategy.

The conduct of VU's president, its director of development, and the few trustees who were privy to Megabucks' plan, is ambiguous from a legal point of view. While they possessed information concerning the potentially conflicting interests, none of them derived any financial benefit from influencing the policy change. Whether or not the nondisclosure caused harm to the university or interfered with the pursuit of its legitimate objective is unclear. The other officers and trustees might well have concluded that the university benefited by the policy change—both on its merits and because of Megabucks' future largesse (by not doing so, VU might have lost the benefits of appreciating real estate values and a substantial gift to the university).

It is unlikely, therefore, that a duty of loyalty violation would be found. But the complicity of directors and officers may have breached the duty of care by not informing their fellow directors, even though they derived no personal benefit from Megabucks' misconduct. Because of the difficulty in ascertaining what, if any, harm to VU might develop as the consequence of its new policy, the imposition of liability on either the director of development, the president, or the fellow trustees resulting from a duty of care violation seems remote. (It should be noted that, because of the conflicting interests present, the business judgment rule could not apply and a more searching inquiry under ordinary duty of care standards might be undertaken.)*

Doing Well by Doing Good: A Conflict of Interests Transaction

Excess Foundation, a private foundation with a diversified portfolio of sound, blue-chip investments valued at $55 million, owns all the outstanding stock of EX Company, which has a major share of a highly specialized electronics business. The foundation carries the EX stock on its books at a value of $35 million, although EX's annual sales exceed $200 million and its average operating income for the last five years was more than $12 million. During this same period, the total dividends paid by EX Company exceeded $2 million only once and have averaged $1.8 million.

The foundation is governed by a five-person board of directors: the chief executive officer of EX, its chief financial officer, two retired senior officers of EX, and the foundation's general counsel. Virtually all of EX's facilities are located in Lufton, a medium-sized Sunbelt city, where it is a major employer and where all directors, except the general counsel, live. Senior officers and directors of EX and the foundation are widely regarded as local business and civic leaders. The Foundation's contributions of several million dollars annually,

---

*The relationship between a breach of duty and the imposition of liability is discussed fully in chapter 6.

primarily for higher education, are distributed throughout the United States.

The foundation has a compliance problem with the excess business holdings provisions of the Internal Revenue Code, which limit the proportion of a business that a foundation may own. However, the foundation's directors would like to satisfy those legal requirements by gifts of a little more than half of the EX stock to several public charities in order to reduce the foundation's 100 percent ownership of the stock to the required level. Such an arrangement would leave the foundation with almost 50 percent of the EX shares and continued working control over EX since the remainder would be held by a number of different nonprofit agencies.

The state attorney general has expressed concern about what he regards as a conflict of interest in the foundation's continued retention of EX stock as a means of perpetuating the foundation's control of EX for the benefit of EX officers, while depriving the foundation of a much greater return on an undervalued asset. He is seeking the divestiture by the foundation of all of the EX stock, which, based on his staff's review of EX's Forms 990 PF (the annual financial return filed with the Internal Revenue Service and most states), he believes is worth substantially more than its book value.

The foundation has never had its interest in EX evaluated, except for purposes of meeting the annual foundation payout requirement. Such assessments tend to value assets on a conservative basis so as not to impose an unnecessarily high distribution requirement. The attorney general is of the opinion that the foundation would have much more money available for grant-making if it sold EX Company and invested the proceeds in a diversified portfolio. The foundation has sought to justify its proposal to give away slightly over half of the stock, in part by arguing that the continued control of EX by the foundation would keep the local economy healthy.

It is not clear that any of the foundation's five directors has the type of conflicting interest covered by the typical conflicts statute. Most conflicts statutes have a limited function; they modify the old common law rules regarding the voidability of contracts involving a conflict. As a result, these statutes are intended to deal only with transactions in a narrow sense. Here, there is no contract or other transaction contemplated by the foundation. A gift or series of gifts to publicly supported charities of the foundation's EX stock, regardless of the underlying motivation, are not the contracts or transactions contemplated by the typical self-dealing statute. Even if they were, no conflicting interest arises directly from the gift: no director or officer sits on the board of any prospective donee organization or has any other interest in the proposed recipients of the foundation's generosity (even if there were common directors, merely having common directors does not necessarily constitute a legal conflict where a personal financial interest is lacking).

In all likelihood, this situation would not bring into play the typical statutory provision regulating conflicting interests (which requires disclosure of the conflict and approval of the transaction by disinterested directors). Nevertheless, serious conflicts issues remain. The interest of at least two of the trustees—EX's CEO and its chief financial officer—are substantial; all the direct and indirect pecuniary benefits (from base salary to incentive compensation to pension plan) that senior corporate officers typically enjoy.

The security of their continued employment and the tangible and substantial benefits associated with that employment are dependent entirely on the foundation's control of EX Company. The decision to retain control, to the extent it may conflict with the foundation's interest in realizing the full value of its holdings, presents a potential conflict between the foundation's interests and the managers' personal financial interests. In a situation such as this, there is an ever-present tension between the needs of the foundation for maximizing income through increased dividends to further its charitable purposes, with the legitimate needs of EX to conserve working capital. The latter factor alone would tend to keep distributions to the foundation as sole stockholder to a modest scale.

While the two current EX officers are faced with the clearest conflict of interest, other board members also may have conflict problems. Merely being a former employee should not evoke the charge of a conflict, although being a pensioner or recipient of deferred compensation might alter that conclusion, depending on how substantial the financial rewards are and whether or not the pension or other deferred income was contingent in any way on the company's financial performance or the actions of fellow directors or officers.[96] Finally, even though the Foundation's general counsel might generally be deemed to be independent—his position as counsel is in no way enhanced or jeopardized by either the retention or the disposition of the EX shares—there are relationships that tie him to EX's executives (although he does not represent EX).[97]

A number of the cases in states without specific statutes on this subject, and in cases arising prior to the adoption of a statute or where broader "loyalty" issues were involved, give some guidance by discussing the factors that a court is likely to focus on in reviewing any such transaction. They are typically: disclosure, disinterested approval, and demonstrable fairness.

The disclosure requirement is straightforward and would require here that all material facts about (1) the proposed dispositions of EX Company stock to the various public charities, and (2) the directors' respective interests be presented to the board (or a committee of the board or independent legal counsel). Such disclosures should include an indication of the range of values that might be achieved through the sale or other disposition of the foundation's interest in EX. It would also include some description of the financial benefits that would accrue to the charitable recipients of the proposed gifts of EX shares and, finally, quantify the financial interests of the directors, assuming their continued employment by EX and/or their eventual retirement.

Whether or not the required disinterested approval can be obtained is a difficult issue to resolve clearly. Under most statutes, each board member may well have the requisite disinterestedness. In any case, the transaction could be approved by showing its fairness. However, if challenged, the directors would bear the burden of establishing fairness.

The potential lack of objectivity of the directors in this case remains troubling. Here, two of the board members—the CEO and chief financial officer—clearly have a substantial direct financial interest in the continued retention of control of EX by the foundation; two others—the retired senior officers—also might have a conflict, depending on the nature of their retirement compensation. Even the foundation's general counsel could be viewed as less than objective because of his long association with EX's senior officers. Even if counsel's independence is established, interested transactions in most cases may not be approved by a single director.

Because of the compromised positions of all the potential decision makers, establishing the fairness of the proposed transaction is essential. This can be accomplished most effectively by hiring disinterested experts—investment bankers, appraisers, business brokers, or other similarly skilled professionals—to examine and render an opinion on the value of EX Company. Given the size of the foundation and the magnitude of EX's business, the expense of such a valuation, while substantial, would be justified so long as it is generally consistent with customary charges for such services.

If, as the attorney general believes, the study will reflect a valuation in the $100 million range for EX, little latitude would be left the directors in choosing a proper course of action. Because the Internal Revenue Code requires annual grants to equal 5 percent of a foundation's assets—$7.75 million in this case—the directors, to defend their original plan, would have to justify foregoing a likely minimum distribution to charity of almost $8 million annually (an increase of more than $3 million each year from current levels).

The continued retention of EX stock—an investment without a ready market—would not be a satisfactory alternative. Its retention would preclude increased charitable distributions by the foundation due to EX's need to retain earnings for working capital or would require forced sales by the foundation of other portfolio securities to meet the increased payout requirement resulting from an increase in the foundation's market value. If dividends were kept at modest levels, the distribution requirements imposed by the Internal Revenue Code inevitably would be violated. Only if the current book value of the EX shares—$35 million—could be sustained during the valuation process would the directors have a plausible argument favoring donating the EX shares and preserving their control.

The board, however, has considerable latitude in fashioning an appropriate disposition. In addition to arm's-length transactions with third parties, it could seek to preserve local control by selling the foundation's interest in EX to an employee stock ownership plan

(ESOP) or a management group via a leveraged buyout (LBO).* So long as the foundation receives demonstrably fair value for its interest, as determined by independent experts, the identity of the purchaser is unimportant. What would be objectionable is for the directors to receive something of great value for themselves—continued control—with no corresponding benefit to the foundation. In addition to retaining experts to evaluate the transaction, the board would be well advised to retain independent legal counsel to negotiate the terms of any disposition to such EX "insiders."

In evaluating the potential outcomes, the directors may consider nonfinancial objectives (such as ethical considerations and public welfare objectives). A business corporation, like EX Company, has a single goal—the so-called "economic objective"—which may be modified by shareholders (for example, they might decide to give a larger proportion of pretax revenues to charity rather than retaining them for working capital or future dividends). Thus, the foundation, as the sole shareholder of EX, could give some weight to the effect on the local economy of a sale of EX to an outsider. The foundation, however, may not modify its pursuit of economic objectives solely to enhance the private interests of its managers, but only to further some legitimate interest of the foundation (for example, maintaining a healthy economy if a purpose of the foundation were to support local cultural and civic events).

The issue, therefore, would be whether the pursuit of a social objective in this particular case (keeping ownership local) in fashioning a disposition is a proper concern of the foundation. Any such concerns should not affect the foundation's principal interest: enhancing its capacity for philanthropy by increasing its resources via an economically favorable disposition. With two roughly comparable alternatives, the foundation might favor a sale to insiders (due to its potential for achieving other legitimate corporate objectives), but it could not do so at a substantial cost to the foundation's chief objective. Doing so would subject the directors to suit by the attorney general and, ultimately, liability, either because the attorney general

---

*The interest of two EX officers in an ESOP or LBO could lead to "self-dealing" problems under the Internal Revenue Code.[98]

would sue for injunctive relief restraining the original board proposal to give away more than half of the shares or because of the financial losses to the foundation from an economically disadvantageous sale or other disposition of the EX shares (i.e., the potential multimillion dollar loss to the foundation's endowment arising from gifts of the EX stock, rather than a sale).

Self-dealing conduct by the foundation directors probably would preclude both corporate indemnification and protection of a D&O policy, thus exposing the directors to a serious risk of liability and financial loss if they chose to proceed with their original plan.

The Duty of Obedience

Significant litigation generated by alleged breaches of the duty of obedience and extensive literature on the subject make this third duty an important concern to nonprofit organizations and their directors.[99]

The Importance of Obedience to Nonprofits

Nonprofits are organized to achieve some specific objective: to help some afflicted constituency, to restore an architectural treasure, to advocate a cause, etc. People generally do not set up charities to pursue a "general purpose," except, perhaps, for private foundations which may distribute funds broadly across the spectrum of charitable activities. Thus, for nonprofits the means and the mission are inseparable. There are at least as many cases dealing with directors' duty of obedience as there are with the standards of care and loyalty. A court may still say, "What more formidable cause of action could exist than the assertion that the trustees are failing to carry out the mandates of the indenture under which they operate."[100]

The Legal Rationale and Limitations

The duty of obedience is akin to that of a trustee administering a trust in a manner faithful to the expressed wishes of the creator.[101] A director is charged with carrying out the purposes of the organization, as expressed in the legal documents creating and defining its mission. At least part of the explanation for this lies in the perception that "donations . . . to [charitable] corporations are made in reliance upon the fulfillment of those charitable purposes,"[102] and that diversions of corporate resources to other goals, no matter how laudable, are not legally justifiable.[103]

Although the purposes may be identified in the charter or by-laws of the organization, they are likely to be amplified in other documents such as the organization's application to the Internal Revenue Service for recognition of its exempt status and in communications, whether public solicitations or grant proposals, in which the organization makes representations about its activities.[104]

The practical importance of the duty of obedience is reflected in the attention charities give to defining and evaluating their "mission." This emphasis on mission statements and the unique way the mission is defined for every organization underscores the distinct nature of nonprofit corporations.[105]

Charitable organizations are organized, operated, and exist to conduct specific activities and confer particular benefits on the public (or at least some significant segment of it).[106] The perpetuation of those particular activities is central to what charities are all about.[107]

Unless allowed by law, nonprofit directors may not deviate in any substantial way from the duty to fulfill the particular purposes for which the organization was created. Such directors, however, may have considerable latitude in determining precisely how such purposes can best be fulfilled.[108] In some circumstances, significant changes in the activities of an organization may be initiated by the directors.[109]

The concept of obedience to the purposes expressed in governing documents reflect an underlying reality; private funds given to support particular activities account for a substantial share of the revenues of nonprofit organizations.[110] The ability to tap such resources is dependent on the confidence that donors have in the faithfulness of those ultimately responsible for managing them. If individuals, foundations, corporate grant-makers, or others believed that an organization was not going to use funds for the purposes intended, those funds probably would not be forthcoming.[111]

The Duty of Obedience and "Law-Compliance"

"Law-compliance" imposes on all directors an obligation to act in conformity with all laws generally affecting the organization. This means that the organization must conduct its activities lawfully.[112]

Some law-compliance obligations affect virtually all nonprofits (for example, the duty to assure compliance with withholding and employment tax requirements); others (for example, the duty to comply with state solicitation laws) would affect only institutions soliciting funds from the public).[113] Directors can assure law compliant behavior by their organization by establishing procedures that they can monitor that comply with applicable laws.[114] However, while directors are charged with assuring law compliance in areas of obvious significance (for example, education laws for schools, and health laws for hospitals), they are not liable for assuring full technical compliance with all regulations (for example, some minor violation of a building code).

In a typical case, there might be several law compliance issues that could be examined by the board to determine if the procedures in place for assuring compliance are adequate and whether any problems in this area exist. (For example, were mandatory financial reports filed on a timely basis with various agencies, such as the IRS, or was there confirmation that the organization maintained favored tax status as a "publicly supported" charity and did not engage in prohibited lobbying?) Assuring compliance is not just a matter of complying with the duty of obedience, but extends also to the care directors take in carrying out their responsibilities.

Case Study: the Duty of Obedience

Ghettos as Gardens: Board Responses to Changing Circumstances and the Duty of Obedience

The Garden Society was established in Megalopolis in 1890 to "collect and diffuse useful information on all topics relating to the culture of plants, flowers, and vegetables and to promote a taste for the same." Its activities have evolved from being a repository of horticultural information to that of an active participant in the life of the community. The society currently deploys the specialized learning and skills of its staff and members to give access to the natural world to poor children and others. A wide range of programs furthers this goal.

Prior to the 1960s, the society was known chiefly for its extensive library of 35,000 volumes used mainly by amateur gardeners and serious horticultural scholars. The collection included many rare books of value not just to horticulturists, but to students of printing and the arts. It is now housed in the society's six-story townhouse. With the escalating cost of insurance and the expense of book preservation, it has become increasingly difficult to maintain the collection.

After reviewing the society's long-term financial goals and prospects, and examining its "mission," the society's board of trustees has decided to dispose of its entire collection except for a working reference library of 11,000 volumes. Following a lengthy review of potential ways of selling the collection, the society has identified as the buyer a major university with a particularly strong program in botany and plant sciences. The sales price is $1.9 million. Thus, the society's objective of preserving and providing scholarly and practical knowledge through the collection would be perpetuated. The proceeds would be used to create an endowment, the income from which would help sustain other society programs. (The society owns its building, which has a fair market value of $2.3 million.)

A number of the society's trustees have objected to the sale of the library, which they view as integral to the society's fulfillment of its long-standing mission. They have charged that their fellow trustees, if they go through with the sale and devote the proceeds to other programs, will have abandoned the society's purposes to pursue goals that are worthwhile, but unauthorized by the society's charter. These trustees have sought the support of the state attorney general. Have the trustees who have voted to sell the society's collection and use the proceeds for other activities breached their duty of obedience to the society and, if so, may they be held liable for such action?

The duty of obedience obligates directors to see that the organization pursues the purposes for which it was created, as expressed by its charter and other governing instruments. Here, the society's purposes, as set out in its charter are quite broad, affording directors substantial latitude in interpreting and applying them.

Safeguarding the "mission" is a critical aspect of nonprofit directors' responsibility to oversee the management of the organization's affairs. That responsibility, however, does not require a rigid and formalistic adherence to outmoded purposes so long as the general goals expressed in the charter are being fulfilled. The society is not directed specifically to maintain a horticultural library or collection. (If it were, the choices confronting the board would be quite different). Its overriding objective—the dissemination of horticultural knowledge—can be pursued in a multitude of ways, all equally appropriate. The decision of how specifically that goal should be pursued is one that corporate law entrusts to directors. Purposes inevitably must be adapted to circumstances that change over time. Thus, making the natural world more accessible to poor inner-city children or encouraging tree planting programs in an inner city neighborhood are valid ways to diffuse knowledge about the "culture" of plants and promote a "taste" for the natural world.

While it always emphasized its renowned library, the society has pursued other ways to diffuse knowledge about horticulture. Like many organizations, it started some programs and terminated others; at different times, varying proportions of its budget were devoted to different aspects of its activities. These were precisely the decisions about the allocation of resources and major plans and policies that directors are required to make.

Nevertheless, the duty of obedience sets some outer limits on what directors may do. While the directors are given considerable discretion in interpreting and applying the broad language of the charter, they may not subvert these purposes or act contrary to them. Because the meaning of language in a charter is partly subjective, courts will not unduly constrain the directors in adapting its purposes. But directors may not disregard clear objectives even if they do so to further perfectly worthwhile goals. For example, had the directors concluded that horticultural activities no longer conferred any substantial public benefits, but that large-scale slum clearance was a better way to use the society's resources, or that promoting commercial agricultural cooperatives would do more good for the public, such decisions would violate the directors' duty of obedience. But changes in the forms of attaining the same broad ends would not violate the directors' duty of obedience.

In the typical cases where the duty of obedience has been violated and, therefore, a corporation's actions exceed its powers (what the law calls "*ultra vires*" activities), a court will grant injunctive relief halting the unauthorized activity and compelling the organization to conduct its activities properly. Although the imposition of financial liability on a director or officer directly for a breach of the duty of obedience is unlikely, directors authorizing *ultra vires* activities may be liable if the result of their conduct leads to some other injury or loss to the organization.

In the society's case, had the sale been prohibited by a court at the request of dissenting trustees as a violation of the society's charter and, therefore, a breach of the directors' individual duties of obedience, the university purchaser could sue the society for breach of contract. If the society lost that suit, it would incur a monetary liability to the university for breaking its contract. Any resulting payment of damages by the society to the university would be a direct result of the assenting directors authorizing the sale of the library in violation of its charter. In such a case, they might be exposed in a subsequent suit by the attorney general or a dissenting trustee, to liability for the loss to the corporation because they were careless in permitting the society to enter into a contract at variance with its mission, i.e., in breach of the duty of obedience. However, the society could indemnify the directors' legal expenses so long as their actions in authorizing the sale had been in good faith (which seems likely here) and no self-dealing or conflict of interests was involved. Any indemnification payment by the society to its directors would be covered by D&O insurance.*

Breach of a duty by a director does not necessarily lead to the imposition of liability on a director with the obligation to pay money damages (or provide other relief). Nor does a finding of liability mean a director alone must bear the costs of any such violation of his duties. The relationship between these duties and any eventual liability arising from their breach is discussed fully in the next chapter. Ways in which organizations and directors can protect themselves through indemnification and insurance from the financial consequences of liability are discussed at length in the concluding chapter.

---

*The legal issues of liability and indemnification/insurance are discussed fully in the two succeeding chapters.

Chapter 5

WHY DIRECTORS GET SUED

The threat of liability has haunted the nonprofit community for years. The literature on nonprofit directors and their legal liabilities has a chronic refrain that potentially disastrous liabilities for nonprofit directors loom just beyond the horizon. Over the years that threat, exacerbating the generalized fear of lawsuits, has been used in an attempt to stimulate more responsible behavior by those who hold leadership positions in nonprofit organizations. The underlying assumption seems to have been that compulsion was the only means of encouraging the evolution of more active and involved directors.[1]

A recent wave of legislative activity however, may have dramatically shifted the balance in favor of directors by significantly curtailing the possibility of director liability.

How Liability Arises

Liability occurs in three distinctly different situations.[2] First, directors may be liable for breaching the duties—care, loyalty, and obedience—that they owe to the corporation if, as a result of the breach, the corporation has been injured. These fiduciary duties may be enforced only by the organization or someone acting on its behalf—fellow directors and officers, members, if any, the state attorney general, and, in some cases, individuals with a special interest in the organization (in actions generally referred to as derivative actions). Second, those dealing with an organization may suffer some personal or financial injury and, in addition to, or instead of, seeking relief from the organization exclusively, may seek to hold directors responsible as individuals. These suits, instituted by those outside the organization, are generally referred to as third-party actions. Third, directors may be personally subject to the requirements of particular statutes, the violation of which will subject them to liability in actions brought by governmental authorities.

Enforcing Directors' Duties

The major source of potential liability for directors arises from the performance of their duties to the organization of obedience, care, and loyalty.[3] Legal actions challenging the performance of directors, whether initiated by members, other directors, an attorney general or, occasionally, others, are considered to be actions brought on behalf of the organization itself for an injury (financial or otherwise) to it.

However, the universe of those legally entitled to commence these actions (known legally as having "standing" to sue) is a small one in most states and the circle of actual plaintiffs generally is even smaller than the law permits. In most states, only the attorney general, directors, or members[4] may bring such actions.[5] Unlike the typical social or fraternal organization, most charitable organizations have no members. Directors, although legally qualified to sue their fellow directors, generally exhibit some reluctance to do this. A New Jersey court, in reviewing voting rights in a large nonprofit membership organization, observed that despite courts' usual reluctance to interfere with the essentially contractual nature of members' relationships with their association, public policy required judicial intervention because individual members (this would apply equally to directors) have no "real," i.e., economic, stake in the management of a nonprofit. Thus, the court said, "[t]here is little to motivate any individual to scrutinize management." This is also true for most public charities, where "members" would rarely risk the loss of dues or suffer poor services.[6]

That leaves a state's attorney general as the enforcing agent. By both common law and statute, the attorney general is consigned the duty of protecting the public's interest in nonprofit organizations, particularly those which are charitable.[7] Staffing problems and the government's relative lack of interest in policing nonprofits have changed little since a 1977 report observed that "proper supervision is hampered in most states by a critical lack of supervisory personnel."[8] In the majority of states, the attorney general lacks a full-time staff lawyer to monitor the area.

This situation remains largely unchanged today. In 1985, for example, only thirteen states reported a total of thirty-three lawsuits brought by attorneys general involving charities at all, and a number of these dealt with professional fund-raisers, fraudulent charities, and with legislative and other initiatives entirely outside the law enforcement area. Only a handful of matters reported raised any questions concerning the conduct of officers and directors.[9]

There have been exceptions to the notion of limited "standing" over the years. Each time a *Sibley Hospital* case (permitting hospital patients to call directors to account)[10] or a *Wilson College* case (allowing college students to proceed against trustees)[11] is announced, it is either heralded as the long-awaited transcendence of the limitations on standing, which many have seen as an effective impediment to greater accountability in the nonprofit area,[12] or it is greeted by a chorus of concern about the potential flood of litigation about to inundate the nonprofit community.

Yet, the major brake on more widespread enforcement of directors' duties continues to be the courts' traditionally narrow view of who may bring such actions. The *Sibley Hospital* and *Wilson College* cases fall within relatively well-established exceptions to the general limitations on standing, and, although much cited in legal commentary, have been followed by very few similar cases. In these "exceptional" cases, the facts brought to the attention of a court by those seeking redress usually were so indicative of wrongful action that the courts strained to give plaintiffs standing. A restrictive approach on the doctrine of standing, however, still seems to prevail in most states.[13]

Even with a relaxation of the restrictions on standing, a great deal of nonprofit litigation would appear unlikely unless there are sufficient economic incentives created for pursuing such litigation. The profit motive is the force that drives most economic activity in the United States, including civil litigation. While a zeal for principled reform may stimulate some litigation, any substantial increase in litigation can only be forthcoming if there are economic rewards for the lawyer, if not the client.[14] The traditional American rule on "fee-shifting," under which each party to a legal contest pays its own legal fees, does not provide any such incentive. The relatively modest economic resources of many nonprofits makes them less than attractive targets.

When all of these obstacles to successfully mounting a lawsuit are finally surmounted, the results still generally favor directors. Even in situations involving self-dealing and a substantial loss to the organization, courts tend not to impose harsh penalties on volunteer directors for their actions or inaction. For example, in one case, a transfer by the trustees of a charity's only asset to a business enterprise controlled by several of the trustees for an inadequate price invoked only a penalty on a single individual, compelling her to restore a modest amount of the dividends she had received.[15] In another case of self-dealing, involving the appropriation of a corporate opportunity for personal gain by the organization's former president, the court simply required a reconveyance of the property improperly acquired.[16] And, in a third, the court, while holding negligent directors accountable for lost income on uninvested assets, sent the case back to the trial court to determine what the organization's cash needs were during the relevant period before concluding how much of the uninvested cash really was surplus and, therefore, could be invested (despite the attorney general's attempt to have a harsh penalty imposed).[17]

In three related decisions, involving the appropriation of a corporate opportunity (a captive insurance company), by officers and directors of a New Jersey automobile club, the courts, while recognizing the action of these directors as a blatant breach of trust, sharply limited the damages, permitting those who benefitted for years from the misappropriated corporate opportunity to pay only a modest price for enjoying its benefits.[18] In another case, involving a diverted corporate opportunity, the errant president merely had to reconvey the property.[19] Even a seeming anomaly, in which a federal court, in applying California law, expounded a strict trust standard as an absolute bar to self-dealing between a controlling foundation trustee and his wholly-owned business, the only party who actually suffered was the federal Small Business Administration, which forfeited its security interest in the foundation assets because it had extended credit to the trustee, knowing the security represented foundation, and not personal, assets.[20]

When there have been serious, but nonvenal derelictions, courts have been loath even to criticize. A Connecticut court, while declining to compel the trustees of a museum to upgrade security, noted that "some measures for improvement as to fire detection and security should be considered," adding that no funds were currently available for such purposes. It suggested, however, that when funds became available, injunctive relief, mandating improved security, might be a proper remedy, thus implying at least some degree of concern about the wisdom of the trustees' prior conduct.[21]

There simply is no hard data to support the conclusion that nonprofit directors have been subject recently to more claims, despite reports of an explosion of liability. A special gubernatorial commission in New York State recently observed that, in contrast to stockholder and other claims against business corporation directors, "there has been no comparable rise in claims against not-for-profit officers and directors."[22] An informal survey conducted among more than two dozen lawyers with extensive nonprofit practices confirms this.[23] Of those surveyed, none reported any claims against the officers and directors of hundreds of client organizations during the preceding five years. Such results hardly suggest an actual liability crisis.

Nevertheless, even relatively infrequent instances of liability have influenced director conduct significantly, given the uncompensated service of the typical board member and the lack of any other material rewards to offset a potentially unfavorable outcome, however remote. (It should be remembered that for every reported lawsuit, many others are settled, some undoubtedly at a cost to directors or to their organizations, even if indemnification and adequate insurance are available).

Third-Party Lawsuits

Third-party lawsuits, while well established in the law, are an exception to the prevailing legal rules. Generally corporate officers and directors enjoy substantial immunity from liability to third persons arising from the acts of an organization that are performed by its agents and employees. A chief attribute of the corporation, nonprofit and for-profit, has been the protection of limited liability that it confers on its owners and managers.[24]

Breach by directors of their fiduciary duties does not provide a basis for claims by third parties, although third parties sometimes advance such contentions to enhance their bargaining power in negotiating a settlement.[25] Summarizing prevailing law, one study flatly states: "The duty of care standards . . . involve duties owed directly to the corporation . . . [and are] not intended to create new third-party rights (e.g., for tort claimants or government agencies) against directors or officers."[26] Similarly, "the duty of loyalty will normally extend only to the corporation."[27] In short, those dealing with an organization have no claim against the directors for mismanagement or self-dealing. Even in the occasional cases where third parties are permitted to challenge directorial misconduct, the relief awarded by the courts, while, perhaps, incidentally benefitting claimants, confers its primary benefit on the organization itself.[28]

What "limited liability" means is that corporate officers and directors are generally liable neither for the performance (or nonperformance) of corporate contracts nor for corporate debts or other corporate obligations.[29] Those dealing with an organization at arm's length (suppliers, customers, lenders, etc.) may look only to the credit of the organization and not to those who control its activities, its officers and directors. However, individual directors (but more typically officers), although they may be acting in a corporate capacity, may have assumed contractual liability if they personally receive something of value outside the contract[30] or if they have made misrepresentations in connection with a contract.[31]

Immunity from contractual liability also may evaporate if it is discovered that the organization has less then a bona fide independent existence. Such discovery is known as "piercing the corporate veil." When the corporation is merely the alter ego or conduit of a dominating personality, the limited liability permitted by the corporate form will not apply. To pierce the corporate veil, two distinct requirements must be met: there must be no corporate existence separate from the dominant individual, and failure to pierce the veil would permit fraud or obvious injustice.

In deciding whether the circumstances are appropriate for the application of this doctrine, courts look for the presence of several factors denoting the illusory nature of organizational (corporate) independence: (1) failure to maintain adequate corporate records and otherwise comply with corporate formalities; (2) commingling of corporate and personal funds and assets; and (3) the use of corporate assets as personal assets.[32]

Third-party claims arise most frequently in the area of tort liability, for injury to persons or property arising from wrongful—but noncriminal—conduct. The doctrine of limited liability does not immunize directors or other corporate agents or employees from liability arising from the commission of torts. When an injury has been done to persons or property by an incorporated organization, both the individuals directly involved in the commission of the acts causing the injury and the organization itself, under the tort doctrine of *respondeat superior,* may incur liability for damages. Normally, a governing body like the board of directors would be relatively remote from the commission of such acts; officers, however, may be more directly involved, depending on their functions. Nevertheless, the basic law in this area—which necessitates personal participation of an individual in a tortious act[33]—makes tort liability of directors and officers difficult to establish.[34] This, undoubtedly, explains the virtual absence of reported cases involving third-party tort claims against directors.[35]

An example may help show why actual tort liability is rare. If the driver of a delivery van for a nonprofit organization causes an accident resulting in serious injuries to two individuals and property damage, the nonprofit corporation, the driver and, perhaps, the organization's directors may be sued for the resulting injuries and property damage. Generally, the directors could not be held liable because the negligence here, if any, would be that of the driver. However, if the driver's negligence could be attributed to some failure of oversight in the selection, training, and recruitment of drivers generally, or the organization's failure to have an adequate vehicle maintenance and inspection program for its automotive equipment (assuming an equipment failure), the directors might be liable for their failure in overseeing the organization's activities.

Statutory Liabilities

There is a third form of liability that may impinge on directors. The nonprofit corporate form offers no insulation from individual director liability when the corporation is engaged in illegal or fraudulent activities.[36] Individual members of an organization and presumably, directors and officers certainly would be liable where they directly participated in wrongdoing.[37] However, directors incur liabilities in these situations, again not by virtue of their position as directors, but because of the character of the actions in question (thus, someone who commits or directs a criminal act is subject to prosecution for the consequences of that action). Other statutes affecting nonprofit corporations also may expose directors and officers to civil penalties and, in some cases, even criminal sanctions. For example, a number of states impose sanctions on officers and directors for the submission of false or inaccurate information filed in connection with state regulatory and reporting schemes.[38]

Tax laws are of particular concern in this regard. Directors may be held responsible for the violation of withholding tax obligations, for the failure to collect or pay state sales and use taxes, if not otherwise exempt, and—with private foundations—for violation of the self-dealing and other provisions of Chapter 42 of the Internal Revenue Code.[39] The corporate form also may be disregarded and personal liability imposed when corporate managers (such as officers and directors) are responsible for assuring compliance with public health and welfare requirements.[40]

The New Dispensation

Although ultimate liability is unlikely, especially in third-party cases, the defense of even the most tenuous tort claim can generate substantial costs. Although the costs may be borne by the organization rather than the director(s), through corporate indemnification and directors' and officers' (D&O) liability insurance, direct exposure to such costs has increased in recent years because liability insurance is often difficult to obtain.[41]

The insurance crisis, for nonprofit organizations has been especially acute because of their limited financial resources and their restricted ability to pass on the increased cost of "doing business." While there has been no report of increases in derivative-type claims, such as those affecting business corporation directors, there are reports of increased tort claims against nonprofit directors. While much of the evidence for the rise in claims would appear to be anecdotal, insurers generally do not distinguish between liability insurance coverage afforded nonprofits and that available to businesses.[42] Because of the justifiable concern about the potential exposure to any claims by volunteer nonprofit directors and escalating defense costs, a number of states have passed ameliorative legislation for nonprofit directors.[43]

The majority of these new laws are "tort reform" measures intended to shield uncompensated directors from liability to third persons for injuries to persons or property. In commenting on a proposed New York law, a gubernatorial commission expressly stated that the purpose of its proposal was intended only to confer immunity on directors of nonprofit groups for third-party tort claims, except in cases of gross negligence.[44] Similarly, Ohio sought to "confer qualified immunities from civil liability in tort upon uncompensated volunteers."[45] Other statutes, while intending to deal primarily with tort claims, may have a much broader sweep, even if unintended. For example, a new Illinois law provides that "No director . . . shall be liable . . . for damages resulting from the exercise of judgment or discretion in connection with the duties of such directors . . . unless . . . willful or warranted."[46] A new Tennessee law provides that "directors . . . shall be immune from suit arising from the conduct of affairs of such . . . organizations."[47] Finally, states such as Pennsylvania and Washington, have followed the Delaware corporate model by permitting organizations essentially to eliminate monetary liability for duty of care violations without actually changing the required standard of care.

The effects, and even the validity, of this explosion of legislation remain uncertain. There have been no reported cases applying any of the more than one dozen new statutes. The statutes themselves vary substantially from state to state.[48] The principal benefit of these new laws will be to make clear that tort claims should not even be brought against nonprofit directors, except, in some states, in the most egregious cases. As a practical matter, this means that directors cannot be made defendants in a personal injury lawsuit as a means of enhancing its settlement value to the plaintiff.[49] While liability always has been difficult to establish, the costs of vindication could be substantial. Now, at least in some states, claims against directors should be discouraged, if not eliminated, and the costs of insurance, perhaps, correspondingly reduced.[50]

While litigation against nonprofit directors and officers has always been problematic, recent changes in the laws of many states have further shifted the odds in favor of directors. Nevertheless, even a remote chance of liability for volunteer directors poses an unacceptable risk and, thus, creates the need for indemnification and insurance protection.

Chapter 6

PROTECTION: INDEMNIFICATION AND INSURANCE

"Indemnification" means that an organization's resources will be used to pay directors' legal costs, judgments, settlements, etc. Directors' and officers' liability insurance is purchased in advance by the organization to cover the organization's indemnification obligations and any direct costs imposed on directors and officers.

Indemnification and insurance are subjects that are not well understood, even by many lawyers.[1] The relevant law in this area has changed very slowly; significant recent changes have had mostly to do with the cyclical nature of the insurance industry and the cost and availability of insurance.[2] For nonprofits, there has been an almost total absence of distinctive legal issues. There are only a handful of cases that even touch upon the subject of indemnification.[3] Surprisingly, there are no cases that seem to deal with insurance by nonprofits of directors' and officers' liabilities.

Indemnification

The early court cases dealing with indemnification reflected differences of opinion concerning the availability and scope of the right of corporations to indemnify directors.[4] Any uncertainty was resolved when, first New York in 1941, then Delaware, and, subsequently most other states passed laws that legitimized indemnification.[5] In the late 1960s, a second wave of change, again driven by a spectre of increased liability for business directors, swept the country, and there were substantial modifications to many of the prevailing indemnity statutes.

Now, in the mid-1980s, heightened concern about liability is spawning a third generation of statutory indemnity schemes.[6] The recent changes in the nonprofit area, however, tend to immunize directors from liability, rather than expand the protections available via indemnification and insurance. In all likelihood, this has been the case because indemnification is effective only if organizations have the financial resources to back up increased protection whereas extending immunity to directors relieves both directors and the organizations they serve of further expense.

The purpose of indemnification is to provide financial protection to directors (and officers) against expenses and liabilities they may incur in connection with actual and threatened legal proceedings connected to their service to a corporation.[7] The justification for the policy is straightforward: "when both the amount and cost of litigation have skyrocketed, it would be difficult or impossible to persuade responsible persons to serve as directors if they were compelled to bear personally the cost of vindicating the propriety of their conduct in every instance in which it might be challenged."[8]

Until relatively recently, nonprofit organizations have shown less concern with acquiring financial protection from liability for their directors and officers than their business colleagues, whether because, until recent years, charitable immunity doctrines afforded significant protection from liability, or because asset-poor nonprofit organizations simply were not viewed as worth the trouble or expense of suing.[9] Even for business corporations, the consuming concern with liability is a relatively recent phenomenon (General Electric, for example, carried no insurance against such liabilities until the late 1960s).

Indemnification Statutes

State laws on indemnification by nonprofits are considerably more diverse and less developed than are the comparable business provisions. (Thirteen states still have the indemnification provision from the 1964 Model Nonprofit Corporation Act (MNCA),[10] eighteen others basically have the 1969 Model Business Corporation Act (MBCA) version,[11] thirteen others have sui generis provisions, while six still lack any statutory enactment and depend on the vagaries of court decisions.) Nevertheless, the dominant model is one applicable originally to business corporations and adapted—if somewhat imperfectly—to nonprofits.

The discussion of indemnification provisions is based on the prevalent business corporate law framework, with some important caveats.[12] A number of states still have the old 1964 MNCA provisions, which, from a protective perspective, are seriously deficient. Those provisions are merely permissive and give a director no right to be indemnified, even if wholly successful in defending against a lawsuit; they cover only the expenses of a defense, excluding judgments, fines, and even settlements; it is unclear under what circumstances they will cover administrative and investigative proceedings; and they exclude threatened litigation.[13]

How the Indemnification Statutes Work

Although most of the influential statutes permit indemnification in situations other than those explicitly dealt with by statute, directors should assume that the statutory framework largely determines the availability and scope of indemnification; attempts by organizations to provide greater or, at least, different protection from that afforded by the statutes will be of uncertain effect.[14] However, Delaware recently made significant changes in its indemnification statutes in a number of areas, one of which strongly suggests that indemnification plans need not track the specific language of the law, but may afford broader coverage.[15] Other states are considering similar modifications.[16]

Under most statutes, when a director of a corporation has successfully defended himself in a litigation, he is entitled to be indemnified by the corporation for the costs of his defense, even if the success results from the assertion of technical grounds (for example, the statute of limitations) and is not on the merits.[17] This is an unqualified right to indemnification that may be enforced in a court (commonly referred to as mandatory indemnification).

In most other situations, however, directors will not have this absolute right to indemnity. They will be indemnified only if the organization has decided to indemnify its directors in accordance with the statute or chooses to do so in a particular case. Such a decision must be reflected either in the organization's charter, its by-laws, a board action (for example, a board resolution reflected in the minutes), or a contractual arrangement between the corporation and individual directors and officers. This is known as permissive indemnification. When a director does not qualify for indemnification made available to him by the corporation, he may apply directly to a court for indemnification and, in such cases, the court, in effect, takes the place of the corporation in deciding whether a director qualifies for indemnification.

Most of the existing indemnification statutes make a critical distinction between the availability of indemnification in pending or threatened legal actions by third parties—a joint venturer, a grantee, a patient, a law enforcement agency, etc.—and so-called derivative actions—those which involve a right of the corporation itself, usually asserted against its own "faithless" officers and directors to recover from them any loss incurred by it.[18] A number of the cases challenging the conduct of directors assert the rights of the corporation rather than those of a third party seeking to recover something from the corporation. For example, virtually all actions by attorneys general relating to "fiduciary management" (as opposed to the enforcement of charitable solicitation laws) would be considered derivative-type actions because they are brought to protect the organization from harm caused by its own directors or officers.[19] So would most actions by co-directors or trustees and by members.

Generally, indemnification in derivative-type actions is much more circumscribed than in third-party actions. In derivative suits, only the expense of a successful defense may be indemnified, whereas in third-party actions, judgments, settlements, and the expenses of a defense may be covered by indemnification. The reason for this distinction is simple. It would make no sense to permit a derivative action by a member or the attorney general, in which a self-dealing director is required to repay an unlawful loan he procured from the organization, and, concurrently, permit that same self-dealing director to be indemnified out of corporate funds when he had just repaid to the corporation the proceeds of his self-dealing.

Even the limited right to indemnification for the costs of a successful defense, however, may be denied if the director seeking indemnification is held liable to the corporation for the breach of one of the duties discussed in chapter 4.[20] Some states, like New York and California, require court approval of legal and other expenses in settling any derivative-type action. Nevertheless, a number of states now permit indemnification to directors of business corporations, even in derivative actions, if no self-dealing is involved, and Pennsylvania already has extended this to its nonprofit corporations and their directors as well.[21]

When an organization assumes an obligation to indemnify its directors, the prospective recipient must meet standards of conduct similar to, but generally less exacting than those discussed in chapter 4. In general, to qualify for indemnification, a director must have acted in good faith and in the best interests of the corporation (or, at least, not opposed to its interests); if the indemnification sought arises out of a criminal proceeding, the director must not have had reasonable cause to believe his conduct was unlawful.[22] For example, although a well-intentioned, honest, but mistaken approval of an economically disadvantageous transaction might violate a director's duty of care, in most states a director generally still can be indemnified.

If one or more directors ultimately were held liable for an injury to the organization they, presumably, would be entitled to indemnity.[23] Some states, however, such as California, require, as a condition to receipt of indemnification, that the indemnitee comply with the full duty of care standards.[24] Duty of loyalty violations that lead to claims against a director are unprotected because the requisite finding that a director acted "in the best interests" of the organization would be unobtainable.

Most statutes prescribe a procedure for obtaining indemnification, when it is permitted. That procedure basically involves a determination, in each case, that the director or officer seeking indemnification has complied with the applicable statutory standard of conduct. A common element in most of the procedures employed is the independence of the decision-maker, whether it is the full board of directors, a board committee, or a special legal counsel appointed for that purpose. A decision to indemnify (or not) generally may be made by the full board if a majority of the deciding quorum is not involved in the matter, or by a disinterested majority of a board commmittee, or by independent or special legal counsel, selected by disinterested directors (assuming there are some).[25] For organizations with members, members can provide the disinterested approval needed when directors lack the required independence. While some states permit either the full board, a committee, or counsel to act, others, including New York, permit alternatives to full board approval only if the latter is not obtainable (presumably, because too many directors are involved in the same situation).

A key aspect of the whole indemnification process, especially for uncompensated directors of nonprofit organizations, is the ability of boards to shift the defense costs (mainly legal fees) from the challenged director or officer while a legal proceeding is in progress— what the statutes generally refer to as "advancing the costs of litigation." While most statutes provide for advancing such costs, a substantial number do not address the issue and, in such states, it is unclear whether an organization may do so.[26]

Virtually all states require the director receiving advance defense costs to promise to repay any advance if he or she is ultimately determined not to have been entitled to the payments (for example, by virtue of a judicial finding of culpable misconduct). This promise or "undertaking" as it is generally called, need not be secured by collateral but simply is a written promise to repay. A number of states, including New York and those following the MBCA, require the use of the same disinterested decision-making process in deciding to make an advance as in granting indemnification, and hold the director receiving the advance to the same standards of conduct to qualify for its receipt.[27] However, Delaware and Pennsylvania recently eliminated the need for case-by-case determinations of eligibility for advancement of expenses and permit general authorization.[28]

Because the statutory formulations of indemnification change from time to time and revising corporate charters and by-laws to paraphrase the elaborate language may be burdensome, it is preferable, in achieving maximum protection under indemnification statutes for directors and officers, to simply oblige the organization to indemnify its directors to "the fullest extent permitted by law," incorporating that commitment in an affirmative undertaking in the organization's by-laws or charter. However, because such governing instruments can always be amended, consideration should be given to including such an obligation in separate contractual arrangements with individual directors and officers.[29] Although the effect of such contracts is still uncertain, they may afford protection that a statute cannot provide or that a new management may be unwilling to give, especially in those states, like Delaware and Pennsylvania, that clearly have endorsed protection beyond what the statutes afford.

Although indemnification statutes leave gaps in protection that can only be covered by insurance, there are several respects in which indemnification affords superior insulation from liability. The typical indemnification provision in direct, i.e., third-party, actions, permits indemnification against fines and penalties imposed on a director as a result of legal action, including punitive damages (which are regarded as a penalty) and for the expenses of defense in investigative matters. Insurance coverage generally will not cover such expenses. The comfort afforded by indemnification may be illusory if an organization lacks the resources to meet its indemnification obligations. Where such resources are absent, an organization must rely on insurance for protection.

The Need for Insurance

Even with the most extensive indemnification provisions, the need for insurance protection is important for a number of reasons. When an organization is unwilling to indemnify (a newly installed management refuses to protect its predecessors, for example) or unable to indemnify (it lacks adequate resources or is prevented by law from doing so), the purchase of directors' and officers' liability insurance (D&O) can fill these gaps.[30] Most importantly, it relieves organizations of the need to accumulate substantial funds against the eventuality of a claim against directors. The costs of a defense, successful or not, usually cannot be passed on by most charities to the clients who are served by the organization's programs. Insurance, therefore, can play an essential role in preserving scarce resources.

For nonprofits, the financial reasons to purchase D&O insurance remain the most compelling. Unlike many business corporations, nonprofit organizations will often lack the resources to mount a vigorous defense. Most nonprofits could not sustain the cost of a substantial judgment against its officers and directors, which they might be obligated to indemnify. D&O insurance enables the nonprofit to meet its indemnity obligations to directors. It simultaneously protects the directors from the corporation's inability to indemnify if the organization lacks resources or if the directors cannot meet the required standard of conduct, but still may be entitled to insurance protection. From the director's perspective, insurance also affords him protection if the organization determines not to indemnify, even if permitted, thus relegating the director to court enforcement—a long, costly and, perhaps, uncertain remedy.

Finally, indemnity statutes offer only partial protection. Judgments or amounts paid in settlement of derivative-type actions, a significant problem for nonprofits, cannot be indemnified against, at least without court approval. With some important exceptions, they can be insured against. Many statutes preclude indemnity payments, even for expenses, when a director has been adjudged liable or simply found by a court to have breached a duty without actually being held liable.

Unlike the business corporation statutes, a significant minority of states lack specific legal provisions permitting nonprofits to purchase D&O insurance. Nevertheless, in light of the current prevalence of D&O insurance, both for businesses and nonprofits, it seems highly unlikely that any serious question would be raised, either on public policy or other grounds, regarding the legality of its purchase, as once might have been the case.[31]

How D&O Insurance Works

D&O policies typically have two separate parts: one reimburses the corporation for any indemnification payments it makes to directors and officers, and the second provides for direct payments to directors and officers when they are not reimbursed by the corporation.[32] It must be emphasized that D&O insurance affords no protection to the corporation itself for *its own liabilities*. They, presumably, would be covered under a comprehensive general or commercial general liability policy.[33]

Who do these policies protect? The policies generally contain definitions of the corporation or other covered organization. Because a number of the standard policies used for nonprofits are simply adaptations of business policies, these definitions should be reviewed carefully to see that coverage is provided not only to the principal nonprofit organization but also to subsidiaries, affiliates, and related organizations, where, unlike businesses, the relationship often is not determined strictly by stock ownership. This review is particularly important for nonprofit organizations involved in commercial activities through complex corporate structures, where directors may serve on subsidiary or affiliated boards at the request of the principal nonprofit organization.[34]

Similarly, although most policies cover either specifically named officers or all officers and directors, the officers and directors of nonprofit organizations often have distinctive titles (for example, a director may be a "governor" and the chief operating officer may be the "executive secretary"). Thus, care must be taken to assure that the policy mentions by exact title those to be covered.

Virtually all of the policies protect against "loss," a key defined term, which typically includes "damages, judgments, settlements and costs, charges and expenses incurred in the defense of actions, suits or proceedings and appeals." While such a seemingly comprehensive definition protects directors against many contingencies where indemnification affords no protection, such as settlements in derivative-type actions, it does not protect against fines and penalties (including punitive damages), which may be covered by corporate indemnity plans

109

and "other matters uninsurable by law." This last exception from the definition of what would otherwise be an insurable loss refers chiefly to the adverse consequences of an individual's intentional or deliberate wrongdoing. As a matter of public policy, such losses are uninsurable for the obvious reason that the availability of insurance in such circumstances would be a stimulus for misconduct by affording full protection to errant directors. Another noteworthy kind of "loss" that is not insured is the expense of an investigation, the cost of which must be borne by the organization under its indemnification obligation.

A significant change in recent years, and a striking difference from the typical general liability policy that many organizations carry, is the handling of the costs of defending a claim covered by the D&O policy. Unlike a general liability insurance policy (for example, a homeowner's policy), where the insurance company has the duty to defend if a claim is made, D&O insurers pay for a defense by the organization's own lawyers (subject to the insurer's consent to the choice of counsel). Until relatively recently, the cost of defense was not included within the definition of "loss" and, thus, any expense incurred in defending an action was not included within the limits of coverage provided by the policy; in other words, it was an extra expense borne by the insurance company.

But this is no longer the case and, today, with D&O defense costs often running into the hundreds of thousands of dollars, this modification in D&O policies significantly diminishes the value of the policy. With average defense costs of almost $500,000 per claim, the value of a $1 million policy is reduced by almost one-half since the defense costs are considered part of the loss. The inclusion of defense costs as part of the insured "loss" means that legal fees become subject to the deductible, which the organization must pay out of its own resources. This change may favor the early settlement of cases, before substantial legal fees are incurred.

The insurance company, even after consenting to the selection of a defense counsel, will want to be kept regularly informed as to legal costs, to which it must consent although it cannot unreasonably withhold its consent to pay such costs. Directors and officers should also understand that a D&O policy, in most cases, will not cover *all* defense costs because of the requirement which allocates such costs between insured and uninsured parties. The D&O policy will not pick up the allocated defense costs of uninsured parties—typically, the organization (which is not directly covered by the policy, but only is protected to the extent it indemnifies officers and directors). Usually, when claims are made against directors, the organization also is named as a co-defendant and, often, vice versa.

Additionally, certain claims may relate both to matters that *are* insured against as well as matters excluded from coverage (for example, a claim alleging negligence by a director, which is covered, and self-dealing, which is not). Thus, any loss incurred from a settlement or judgment terminating a lawsuit, as well as the expenses of defending it, must be allocated to the insured and uninsured claims. It is the better practice to reach an early agreement with the insurer on such matters of allocation even if, as is often the case, all the defense costs are advanced during the time that the litigation is in progress.

A major concern for nonprofits is how to pay for the defense of a lawsuit. One of the principal purposes of taking out D&O insurance is to be sure that the funds for a defense will be available if needed. Many nonprofits would need to have defense costs advanced. Despite some policy language to the contrary, however, virtually all insurers view the advancement of defense costs to an insured organization as wholly discretionary.[35] Nevertheless, most insurers will advance costs, particularly when the insured is financially unable to mount an adequate defense. Like the allocation problem, this issue should be addressed at the earliest practicable moment (of course, advances must be repaid if an adverse judgment is rendered finding a claim is uninsurable under the policy).

Protection of a D&O policy is broadly defined to cover acts and omissions by insured directors in their official capacity (not, of course, wrongful acts unconnected to service as a director). To be covered, however, a claim against a director arising from the commission or omission of some action must be made during the period of time the policy is in effect. For such "claims made" insurance it does not matter when the action or omission occurred; it matters only when the claim against the director is asserted (in effect, this precludes an organization from purchasing insurance to protect against a known liability and from creating an indefinite exposure for the insurer in the future). All policies today are considered claims made insurance. (At an earlier time, policies covered "wrongful occurrences" regardless of when the related claim was asserted.)

As long as an organization can renew its coverage, "claims made" protection is adequate. But with a tight insurance market, renewal policies, at least on adequate terms, may not always be available. In such a case, organizations can acquire additional protection by exercising their rights under "extended reporting period" or "discovery" clauses. These permit any insured organization, for an additional (and substantial) payment, to extend its coverage, for less than a full term, for claims from covered wrongful acts committed during the original policy period.

Additionally, the exercise of an organization's rights under a "notice" clause provision in a D&O policy affords further protection. A typical notice clause requires the insured organization to give notice to the insurance company of any circumstances known to it that may give rise to a claim. Once this is done, even at the end of a policy period or during its extension through a discovery clause, a claim reported in that notice will be covered, even after the policy expires. It, therefore, is advisable to present a complete list of potential claims at the end of any policy period (although such action may lead to an increased premium). At the same time, any claim included in such a notice would not be covered by a new carrier because most policies exclude claims covered by a prior policy.[36]

Most claims against directors and officers are ultimately settled without a trial. Settlement provisions, therefore, are of particular importance. Most policies require the insurance company's consent to a settlement although the insurer may not unreasonably withhold such consent. This means that the insurer should always be kept fully apprised of all legal developments during the course of a litigation concerning an insured claim.

The list of exclusions from D&O coverage has grown somewhat longer over the years and is one of the major changes from the early D&O policies. Exclusions serve to protect insurers against potentially catastrophic loss (for example, the standard pollution exclusion), matters which are peculiarly within the insured's control (such as libel, slander, and other intentional torts), and those that cannot be adequately evaluated for underwriting purposes. A typical list of exclusions would cover the following:

> Suits alleging directors took actions against the organization's interest for their own personal gain;
> suits seeking the return of unauthorized remuneration;
> suits for personal and property injury, including defamation;
> suits involving dishonest, fraudulent, and criminal acts;
> suits for failure to obtain adequate insurance for the organization's operations, for example, carrying inadequate property damage protection (this prevents the use of D&O policies to make up for lack of other coverage);
> claims covered by other insurance (in which case, the D&O policy will only pick up the excess liability);
> suits for pollution damage;
> suits alleging violations of ERISA;[37]
> suits brought by one insured party (for example, the organization) against another insured party (for example, a director).

When an organization applies for D&O insurance, the application is usually signed by an officer, often the chief executive or other senior officer of the organization. This application becomes part of the organization's contract with the insurance company (legally, insurance policies are treated as contracts). A material misrepresentation in an insurance contract can void an entire policy.[38] The greatest care, therefore, should be taken in completing the application accurately because a misrepresentation or omission by the officer completing and signing the application can deprive totally innocent directors of coverage they believed they had. Nonprofits, with their typical all-volunteer boards, may be vulnerable to this problem if there is a "faithless" executive director or other senior officer whose functions include obtaining D&O coverage. To some extent, this risk can be minimized by having the directors execute separate applications and seeking the inclusion of language in the policy (usually the "severability clause") affirming the separate nature of the D&O insurance policies for each director and officer.

Gaps in D&O Coverage

Even with a comprehensive indemnification program, backed up by insurance, some gaps in protection for directors remain. The principal shortcomings are the lack of protection from judgments and settlements in derivative-type actions where directors are accused of self-dealing or conflicts of interests (*not* negligence) and from claims involving dishonesty and intentional misconduct due primarily to the historical public policy against coverage in such cases. This may change if more states do as Pennsylvania has and permit indemnification in derivative actions.

However, the most troublesome concern with D&O coverage is the cost of protection. When D&O insurance premiums, prior to the mid-1980s, were still quite modest, the protection afforded by insurance seemed prudent. As the cost of D&O insurance for (cash-starved) nonprofits has trebled and quadrupled, countervailing arguments, especially given the remoteness of an ultimately unfavorable outcome, have appeared more plausible. Nonetheless, the alternative of self-insurance (effectively, "going bare") for many nonprofits is unrealistic in light of the havoc that defending against even a frivolous claim could wreak on a precarious budget, at least so long as the organization was obligated to indemnify its directors (volunteer directors generally insist upon it). The likelihood is that nonprofits, so long as they can pay the D&O premiums, will and, in most cases, should continue to do so.[39]

For some organizations, however, with relatively little interaction with the public (for example, private foundations whose "activities" consist primarily of managing investments and awarding grants), D&O policies may be regarded as a dispensable luxury. On the other hand, for organizations conducting extensive activities, especially those that tend to generate liabilities (for example, hospitals, schools, day-care programs, etc.), eliminating D&O coverage would be inadvisable.

In each case, the board should assess the likelihood (or remoteness) of liability, the magnitude of a potential loss, and the organization's available financial resources to meet any such contingency. With little likelihood of liability and substantial resources, even the prospect of a sizeable judgment might be acceptable. With few resources, the possibility of any substantial exposure is intolerable when its occurrence might spell the demise of an organization or a significant cutback in programs or services.

Alternatives to Insurance

Businesses have been exploring a variety of techniques to provide alternatives to conventional D&O insurance or at least to complement it. These include expansion of statutory rights through adoption of special by-law provisions or through contracts between organizations and their individual directors. Such efforts to extend the permitted scope of indemnification, in some states, may remain subject to challenge on public policy grounds.

The one advantage of contracts, however, is that they afford protection to a director against a change in the organization's management. At the same time, such contracts do not respond to the exigencies of the insurance market. That is why most of these alternative strategems are unavailing for nonprofits: they depend, to a great extent, on an organization's financial ability to protect against risks otherwise covered by insurance.

This is equally true for such widely-discussed, if not employed, initiatives as those involving captive and consortium insurers (insurance companies wholly owned by one or more organizations). In addition, the results of using a captive will be no more favorable to nonprofits in the short run than continued dependence on the vagaries of the market, and, by the time a captive could provide an alternative, the cyclical nature of the insurance crisis might have moderated its impact. There are signs of its having begun to do so already.

Exploring such cooperative arrangements, however, may provide long-range alternatives for nonprofits with some capital (for example, those in the health-care field). Legislative changes in the basis of liability or preclusion of certain types of claims seem to represent a more promising alternative (for example, New York State's Insurance Department already has mandated decreases in insurance rates based on the projected impact of the passage of tort reform proposals).[40]

BOARD LIABILITY

The real problem facing nonprofits is their lack of resources, which makes both the risk of "going bare" and the alternatives to insurance (trust funds, letter of credit arrangements, etc.) unpromising. Most nonprofits will simply have to ride out the storm using more careful risk management and other means of minimizing exposures.

NOTES

All notes are cited in conventional legal form. Sources that are referred to frequently in this book are cited in an abbreviated form, as follows:

Model Nonprofit Corporation Act ("MNCA")—1964

Model Business Corporation Act ("MBCA")—1969

Revised Model Nonprofit Corporation Act ("RMNCA")

Revised Model Business Corporation Act ("RMBCA")

American Law Institute Principles of Corporate Governance: Restatement and Recommendations, Tentative Draft No. 1 ("ALI T.D. #1")

Analysis and Recommendations, Tentative Draft No. 2 ("ALI T.D. #2")

Analysis and Recommendations, Tentative Draft No. 3 ("ALI T.D. #3")

Analysis and Recommendations, Tentative Draft No. 4 ("ALI T.D. #4")

Analysis and Recommendations, Tentative Draft No. 5 "ALI T.D. #5")

All citations to state statutes are derived from the official code of that state, as for instance, to McKinney's 1970 in New York, unless otherwise specified.

Chapter One

[1] IRS, Internal Revenue Code §501 (c)(d)(e) (1954); Cerny & Knap, *Current Issues in the Administration of Tax-Exempt Organizations* 61 (Table 20) (Practicing Law Inst., 1986); Fant, *Doing Well While Doing Good and the Pitfalls of the Unrelated Business Income Tax*, 1985 Taxes-The Tax Magazine, 862, 863; McGovern, *The Changing Character of Exempt Organizations*, The Philanthropy Monthly, April 1986, 19, 20; American Association of Fund-Raising Counsel, *Giving USA: Estimates for Philanthropic Giving in 1985 and the Trends They Show* 50 (1986).

[2] National Center for Charitable Statistics, Support and Revenue and Assets by State 1 (1984) (estimating approximately $160 billion total assets nationwide for nonprofits, excluding religious organizations); G. Rudney, *A Quantitative Profile of the Nonprofit Sector* 12, 13 (Yale University Program on Non-profit Organizations hereinafter "PONPO", Working Paper No. 40, 1981); G. Rudney and M. Weitzman, *Significance of Employment and Earnings in the Philanthropic Sector* 1972–1982 (PONPO Working Paper No. 77, 1983); IRS Exempt Organizations Master File, Breakdown of Section 501(c)(3) Organizations by State, Table I (1980).

[3] *The Non-Profit Sector of the Region's Economy*, III Regional Plan News (1982); D.A. Grossman, L.M. Salamon and D.M. Altschuler, *The N.Y. Nonprofit Sector in a Time of Government Retrenchment* (Urban Inst. Press, 1986)

[4] Hansmann, *The Role of the Nonprofit Enterprise*, 89 Yale L.J. 835, 863; *contra* Starr, *Profit-Making and Nonprofit Organization in Medical Care: The Boundaries of Capitalist Enterprise*, (Draft of Ponpo Working Paper, 1980).

[5] *Commissioner v. Pemsel*, 1891 A.C. 531, 583.

[6] *Bob Jones University v. United States*, 461 U.S. 574, 578 (1983) (citing from a case more than a hundred years old, *Ould v. Washington Hospital for Foundlings*, 95 U.S. 303, 311 [1877]) But *cf.*, *Utah County v. Intermountain Health Care*, 709 P.2d 265, at 269 and 276 (Utah, 1985) (public benefit is not sufficient to qualify for real prop-

erty tax exemption; a donative element is required).

[7] See IRS Form 1023, Application for Recognition of Exemption and Instructions for Form 1023 Under §501(c)(3) of the IRC.

[8] ALI §2.01 (T.D. No. 2, 1984); See also, Sommer, *Keynote Address of Sorts*, 31 Bus. Law. 871, 872 (1976) (quoting Professor [now Judge] Richard A. Posner, "The corporation is primarily a method of solving problems encountered in raising substantial amounts of capital for a venture.").

[9] This accounts for the persistence of the ultra vires doctrine in non-profits and the continuing importance of the duty of obedience, once one of the three great obligations of corporate directors.

[10] Brace, Elkin, Robinson and Steinberg, *Reporting of Service Efforts and Accomplishments* (Financial Accounting Standards Board, 1980) (reporting a study by Peat, Marwick & Mitchell on certain types of nonbusiness organizations' efforts and accomplishments related to the services they were established to provide); National Charities Information Bureau, *Report on Preliminary Test Phase Program on Effectiveness and Efficiency Project 5* (Oct. 1985).

[11] ALI §2.01 (T.D. No. 2, 1984) (all businesses may devote a "reasonable amount of resources to social objectives"); See also Troyer, Slocombe and Boisture, *Divestment of South Africa Investments: The Legal Implications for Foundations*, Other Charitable Institutions and Pension Funds, 74 Geo. L.J. 127, 132 (1985); Campbell & Josephson, *Public Pension Trustees' Pursuit of Social Goals*, 24 J. of Urb. and Contemp. L. (1983).

[12] *Ashton v. Dashaway*, 84 Cal. 61 (1890).

[13] Henn and Boyd, *Statutory Trends in the Law of Nonprofit Organizations: California Here we Come!* 66 Cornell L. Rev. 1103, 1106 (1981).

[14] In fact, the inability of the nonprofit corporation to distribute profit makes it ill-suited as a vehicle for capital formation. This has been a source of tension in certain industries, such as health care, tradition-

ally dominated by nonprofits, in which the need for capital has out-stripped the capacity of the nonprofit provider. The result is an increasing trend toward for-profit organization forms. See P. Starr, *The Social Transformation of American Medicine* (1980); *but cf.*, Clark, *Does the Nonprofit Form Fit the Hospital Industry*, 93 Harv. L. Rev. 1417 (1980).

Chapter Two

[1] Delaware, for example, allows a corporation to have a minimum of one director. However, it has only one statute for business and non-business organizations, and the low minimum may reflect the exigencies of closely held business organizations which often will have one or two shareholder/directors. Many statutes permit corporations to have one or two directors if they are closely held. *See, e.g.*, Del. Gen. Corp. Law §141(b); New York Bus. Corp. Law §702(a). The RMNCA is more typical in fixing a minimum. RMNCA §8.03 (Exposure Draft March 1986).

[2] Smaller companies generally have smaller boards and banks and other financial institutions have larger boards. Korn/Ferry International, *Board of Directors 12th Annual Study*, at 4 (Feb. 1985). There were 633 responses to this survey of the 1,000 largest corporations, which, of course, may not reflect smaller publicly held companies and closely held businesses.

[3] Unterman and Davis, *The Strategy Gap in Not-For Profits*, Harv. Bus. Rev. 30, 30 (May–June 1982); Nova Institute, *Fund Raising Practices of United Way Agencies in New York City*, at 57 (1980) ("[A]gencies that raised the largest total amount of contributions . . . tended to have the largest boards."). This study suggests a reason for the differences that is explored further in Chapter Four.

[4] A. A. Berle, Jr., & G. C. Means, *The Modern Corporation and Private Property* (1932). The proxy fight continues to retain vitality as a means of wresting control of management of a corporation; *see, e.g.* Salpukas, *The Defender of Allegis*, N.Y. Times, June 1, 1987, at D1, col. 3.

[5] There are some notable exceptions: Consumers Union, Friends of the Earth, and a number of other prominent organizations. The use of the electoral process to change control is exceedingly rare (other than, perhaps, in governmentally funded community-based groups where constituent participation may be mandated).

[6] *See, e.g., Creighton Home v. Waltman*, 140 Neb. 3, 299 N.W. 268 (1941) ("Plaintiff's board . . . serve without pay . . . Of necessity, . . . proper administration calls for unselfish, civic-minded service of men of high integrity.") *Midlantic Nat. Bank v. Frank G. Thompson Estate*, 170 N.J. Super. 128, 405 A.2d 866 (1979) ("[T]hose who give of their time for the public good by serving on boards of charitable corporations"). Id. at 871. Even within the foundation community, the compensation of directors, while sometimes substantial, is still the exception. According to a Council on Foundations study, less than one-quarter of foundations compensated their directors and the median payment was under approximately $5,000. Council on Foundations, *1984 Foundation Management Report* (1984). For publicly supported charities, compensation other than payment of the expenses of attendance is virtually unheard of, although nonprofits have long enjoyed the legal right to make such arrangements. *See, e.g.*, N.Y Not-For-Profit Corp. Law §202(12) (nonprofit corporations have the power to "appoint officers . . . fix their reasonable compensation and the reasonable compensation of directors . . .").

[7] *Hot Seats, Board Members Draw Fire, and Some Think Twice About Serving*, Wall Street Journal, February 5, 1986, at 1, col. 1.

[8] Korn/Ferry, *supra* note 2, at 4. The boards covered by the Korn/Ferry Survey reflected an average of four "insider" and nine "outsider" directors.

[9] The National Charities Information Bureau (formerly the National Information Bureau), one of two major donor information agencies, has incorporated in its criteria for evaluating charities a requirement that "members . . . serve without compensation." The sole exception it permits is the "paid staff head." National Information Bureau, *NIB Standards for Philanthropies* 11 (1982).

[10] "Voluntary organizations are very different from . . . business organizations and we only confuse ourselves on responsibilities by trying to see our roles in contexts that don't . . . apply," comments Brian O'Connell on the perceived difference between the CEO of a business and the "chief volunteer officer." B. O'Connell, *The Board Member's Book* 53 (1985).

[11] Only California mandates a disinterested majority; Cal. Corp. Code §§5233(d)(2)(C), 5233(d)(3)(C), 7233(a)(2), 7233(a)(3)(b)(1), 9243(d)(3)(C), 9243(d)(4)(C). The RMNCA includes an optional provision requiring a disinterested majority; RMNCA §8.13 (Exposure Draft March 1986).

[12] While perhaps advisable, as O'Connell suggests and the NCIB and others virtually command, the lack of staff representation on a board can have detrimental effects on an organization and, in the worst case, can permit the dominance of an incompetent, corrupt or even venal chief staff officer. *See, e.g.*, The Washington Post, Jan.18, 1986, at 1, col. 2.

[13] Although directors, in virtually all states can act by written consent, such consent must be unanimous, effectively precluding its frequent use and, because of logistical difficulties, limiting its use to smaller boards, probably seen most frequently in closely held boards. *See, e.g.*, N.Y. Bus. Corp. Law §708(b) (1985).

[14] In some states, alternate board members may be selected if elected directors serve in a representative capacity. This exception underscores the general maxim that Board service is individual and personal and reflects an appreciation of the value of continuity in Board service as a predicate for effective functioning. *See, e.g.*, N.Y. Not-for-Profit Corp. Law §703(d).

[15] *See, e.g.*, Del. Gen. Corp. Law, §141(i).

[16] *See* J. Weber, *Managing the Board of Directors* 4 (1975) (suggesting an optimum size in the thirties to permit creation of an effective committee structure, "[T]he general experience of most . . . organizations suggests 30 to 36 as an optimum size"). *But see*, Karl Mathiasen, *The Board of Directors of Nonprofit Organizations* 10–11 (Management Assistance Group 1977) (pointing out that "most

nonprofit organizations can do with considerably fewer than 30" because "inevitably actual governance will be left to a smaller group"). Service in an advisory capacity may give the board broader perspective when necessary and introduce potential recruits to service without diluting effective governance.

[17] Bishop, *Sitting Ducks and Decoy Ducks: New Trends in the Indemnification of Corporate Directors and Officers*, 77 Yale L.J. 1078 (1968); Subak, *Let's Practice What We Preach*, 40 Bus. Law. xvi (1985) ("Corporations are best governed when their affairs are monitored or overseen by a board of directors that has at least a majority of independent directors.") *Id.* at xvi.

[18] *See e.g., Board Members Draw Fire and Some Think Twice about Serving*, Wall Street Journal, Feb. 5, 1986, at 1, col. 1.

[19] *See e.g.*, International Business Machines, Inc., *Notice of 1985 Annual Meeting and Proxy Statement* 8 (1985) (reporting 92 percent attendance of the board of directors at thirteen meetings), American Telephone & Telegraph Co., *Notice of 1985 Annual Meeting and Proxy Statement* 4 (1985) (reporting 87 percent attendance at twelve meetings), and General Electric, *Notice of 1985 Meeting of Shareholders* 15 (1985) (reporting 93 percent attendance at ten meetings). Out of the total number of directors for all three corporations, only three failed to attend 75 percent of the meetings. Lest one conclude that the cachet of these corporate giants attract members to duty, less glamourous enterprises report comparable results. *Cf.*, Stop and Shop Companies, Inc., *Notice of Annual Meeting of Stockholders* 7, (1985), (reporting that with the exception of one newly-elected director, all board members attended at least three-quarters of the scheduled meetings).

[20] Korn/Ferry, *supra*, note 2 at 5 (1985).

[21] *See e.g.*, A. D. Ullberg & P. Ullberg, *Museum Trusteeship* 47 (1981) ("Committees are essential to the conduct of the business of most boards").

[22] *Statement of the Business Roundtable*, 37 Bus. Law. 2083, 2109 (1978). However, in determining a director's compliance with the "duty of care" when there has been extensive delegation of board

powers, the focus would be on the reasonableness of the delegation. Merely delegating to others some board responsibility, even when the delegation is appropriate, by itself does not discharge the director's duty if the act of delegation is flawed in some way or there is insufficient follow-up.

[23] RMNCA §8.01(b) (Exposure Draft March 1986); RMBCA §8.01(b) (1984); ALI §3.01 (T.D. No. 2, 1984) (allows management "by or under" the board); Cal. Corp. Code §§5210, 7210, 9210(a), 9210(b); N.Y. Bus. Corp. Law §701; Del. Gen. Corp. Law. §141(a). *Contra* NY Not-for-Profit Corp. Law §701(a).

[24] Manning, *The Business Judgment Rule and the Director's Duty of Attention: Time for Reality*, 39 Bus. Law. 1477, 1482; ALI §3.02 (T.D. No. 2, 1984), ALI §4.02 (T.D. No. 3, 1984). This, unfortunately, is clearer for business organizations whose officers are generally full-time employees actually performing the functions of managing the corporation, whereas, for nonprofits, officers are generally board members—with the exception, perhaps, of the chief staff officer—who do not manage the organization, while those who do are not called officers. The need to delegate, however, is no less compelling, and it is unlikely that such problems with nomenclature would be influential with a court. *Santos v. Chappell*, 65 Misc. 2d 559, 318 N.Y.S.2d 570 (Sup. Ct., N.Y.Co. 1971) (employing a functional analysis to determine that the control of a trade association was vested in a board of governors rather than a board of directors, which actually was subordinate to the board of governors).

[25] *American Center for Education, Inc. v. Cavnar*, 80 Cal. App. 3d 476, 145 Cal. Rptr. 736 (1978) ([when] directors are in frequent contact with each other, it is unnecessary to hold formal meetings in order to reach decisions).

[26] ALI §4.03 (T.D. No. 4, 1985). By way of contrast, the audit committee's existence is effectively mandated for virtually all publicly held business corporations. The SEC's Proxy Rules, 17 C.F.R. §240.14a–101, Sched. 14A, Item 6(d)(1) (1986) requires disclosure of the existence of standing audit, nominating, and compensation committees, and a description of their functions and operations. The New York Stock Exchange requires that a company seeking to have

its securities listed for trading on the Exchange have an audit committee comprised exclusively of independent directors. N.Y. Stock Exchange, *Listed Company Manual*, §303.

[27] *See, e.g.*, A. Ullberg & P. Ullberg, *Museum Trusteeship* 47–54 (1981); R. Ingram & Associates, *Handbook of College & University Trusteeship* 69–76 (1980); K. Mathiason, *The Board of Directors of Nonprofit Organizations* (1977). Even critics of the excesses of committees appear to tolerate them. B. O'Connell, *The Board Members Book: Making A Difference in Voluntary Organizations* 85–95 (1985).

[28] ALI §3.03 (T.D. No. 2, 1984); Fredericks, *What Should the Audit Committee Do?* XIX No. 5 Philanthropy Monthly 28–32 (1986); Price, Waterhouse, *The Audit Committee, The Board of Trustees of Nonprofit Organizations and the Independent Accountant*, Publication No. 850313.

[29] ALI §3.06 (T.D. No. 2 1984). Although in the charitable counterparts to closely held corporations—*e.g.*, family controlled private foundations—there are often formal or informal understandings or agreements concerning the nomination and election of directors, such arrangements, while widespread are vulnerable to attack (however remote), especially if internal family squabbles arise. The freedom in ordering the management of a business organization cannot be easily transposed to the nonprofit sector. Although considerable latitude may be afforded stockholders regarding the governance of a business venture because they are private individuals contracting only about their personal rights, that rationale cannot be extended to a charity that has no owners. The directors, even when they are also "members", are fiduciaries for the public served by the organization. Thus, they may not agree in advance to designate a particular individual for board service, particularly where any such agreement purports to bind individuals with no personal interest at stake. Ironically, the clearest exposition of this can be found in a case emanating from the quintessential corporate haven, perhaps precisely because its courts so well comprehend critical, yet often overlooked, distinctions between businesses and nonprofits. *See, e.g., Chapin v. Benwood Foundation, Inc.* 402 A.2d 1205 (Del. 1979) ("The members and trustees [of the foundation] . . . are not stockholders in any

sense. The persons having the beneficial interest in the corporation . . . are those located in the Chattanooga area . . . who will benefit from the periodic decisions of the board."). *Id.* at 1211; *aff'd sub nom. Harrison v. Chapin,* 415 A.2d 1068 (Del. Supr. 1980).

[30] The Uniform Management of Institutional Funds Act (hereinafter "UMIFA"), approved by the National Conference of Commissioners on Uniform State Laws in 1972 has been adopted in twenty-nine states. *See, also,* W. Cary and C. Bright, *The Developing Law of Endowment Funds, The Law and The Lore Revisited,* 1974.

[31] Manning, *The Business Judgment Rule and the Director's Duty of Attention: Time for Reality,* 39 Bus. Law.1477 (1984).

[32] *See* Del. Gen. Corp. Law §141(c); N.Y. Not-for-Profit Corp. Law §712(a). *See also* ALI §4.03 (T. D. No. 3, 1984).

[33] *See, e.g., Attorney General v. Olsen, et al., Trustees,* 191 N.E.2d 132, 136 (Mass. 1963) (the court refused to review the decision of charitable directors to contract with a local bank for investment advice, stating "None of the trustees had much . . . experience in . . . investments, and it was entirely proper for them to seek expert advice."). *But see, Chapin,* 402 A.2d at 1210 (Del. Ch. 1979) ("directors . . . may not delegate . . . duties which lay at the heart of the management of a corporation"), *aff'd sub nom. Harrison v. Chapin,* 415 A.2d 1068 (Del. 1980).

[34] *See, e.g.,* Cal. Corp. Code §§5231(b)(1)–(3), 7231(b)(1)–(3), 9241(b)(1)–(1).

Chapter Three

[1] This point forms the basis of a provocative and important challenge to the conventional wisdom about directors' duties. Manning, *The Business Judgment Rule and the Director's Duty of Attention: Time for Reality,* 39 Bus. Law. 1477 (1984).

[2] The business literature tends to be much more definitive and uniform in its description of key board functions. As elaborated by the ALI, the principal board responsibilities include: (1) selection of senior executives, (2) oversight of corporate conduct to evaluate performance in light of objectives, and (3) review and approval of major plans and actions. Korn/Ferry International, *Board of Directors 12th Annual Study*, at 12 (1985). ALI §3.02 (T.D. No. 3, 1984). This characterization is substantially in accord with those preferred in the *Corporate Director's Guidebook*, 33 Bus. Law. 1591, 1608-10 (1978), and *The Statement of the Business Roundtable*, 33 Bus. Law. 2083, 2096-2103 (1978). It also is consistent with the information reported by board members themselves in identifying the significant issues they deal with as, in order of importance, financial performance and then, depending upon relative size, either strategic planning and issues of succession, or financing/capitalization and merger/acquisition. Even those observers who have been more critical of the somewhat traditional notions of corporate governance and believe that the corporate board is "not placed in center stage" (Vagts, *Directors: Myth and Reality*, 31 Bus. Law. 1227, 1229-30 [1976]) accept the fact that boards, while acting primarily in a "collaborative" relationship with management, nevertheless, exercise some degree of oversight, and remain deeply involved in crisis management involving planning for and managing the problems of succession. *See, e.g.*, Manning, *supra* note 1, at 1484-85.

[3] Some nonprofits have distinctive rules or conventions. For example, in health care institutions, the judgments of staff—*i.e.*, physicians—may be accorded great weight in personnel matters. *Foote v. Community Hospital of Beloit*, 195 Kan. 385, 405 P.2d 423 (1965); American Hospital Association, *Guiding Principles for Governance of the Health Care Institution* 9 (1972).

[4] National Charities Information Bureau, *Report on Preliminary Test Phase Program on Effectiveness and Efficiency Project* 1 (1985); *but c.f.* Brace, Elkin, Robinson and Sternberg, *Reporting of Service Efforts and Accomplishments* (Financial Accounting Standards Board, 1980) (service efforts and accomplishments may lie beyond the capabilities of financial accounting). For further discussion of this issue, see Kurtz, *Non-Traditional Revenue Ventures of Tax-Exempt Organi-*

zations: The Role of Trustees, 39 Rec. of the City of N.Y. B. A. 129 (1984).

[5] Particular requirements for directors' actions will vary somewhat from state to state, although there is substantial similarity.

[6] Despite some rather striking distinctions between business and non-profit corporations, their respective directors appear to donate about the same amount of time and effort to "directing." For example, in 1984 directors spent an average of 121 hours annually on board matters, including travel and preparation, and the five-year average since 1980 was 122 hours. Korn/Ferry International, *supra* note 2, at 21. By contrast, almost one-half of the directors of nonprofit organizations spent 60–120 hours annually, while another quarter spent 120 or more hours yearly. The *The Touche Ross Survey of Business Executives on Non-Profit Boards* 2 (1979). Although the range is apparently much broader than it is for business directors, the average time spent by nonprofit directors approaches that devoted to corporate affairs by their business counterparts. Part of the explanation for this may be that the inactive nonprofit director, if queried, simply did not respond and so the sample of responding directors included only active ones. In the business sector, as we have seen, active participation is the norm. However, nonprofit figures may also be affected by significantly shorter travel time, while the Korn/Ferry report involves only major public corporations with geographically dispersed boards and a necessarily substantial amount of travel time.

[7] According to one scholar, "minutae occupy many board meetings," M. Middleton, *The Place and Power of Non-Profit Boards of Directors* 36 (PONPO Working Paper No. 78, 1983).

[8] Manning arrives at a similar conclusion concerning the tasks performed by corporate business directors. Manning, *supra* note 1 at 1483; B. O'Connell, *The Board Members Book: Making a Difference in Voluntary Organizations* 23–32 (1985); Nason, *Responsibilities of the Governing Board*, in Handbook of College and University Trusteeships 27–46 (1980).

[9] *See generally, The Touche Ross Survey, supra* note 6, at 9–13; M. Middleton, *supra* note 7 at 10–11; K. Mathiason, *The Board of Di-*

rectors of Nonprofit Institutions 2–7 (1977); B. O'Connell, *supra* note 8 at 23–32; Nason, *supra* note 8 at 27–46.

[10] Although publicly held business corporations are considerably larger and more complex than all but the largest nonprofits, nonprofit directors can no more manage their affairs than can their business peers. And, despite the law's strictures, it is widely recognized that that is not the director's proper role. Thus, "the board . . . is not expected to operate the business . . . The responsibility . . . is limited to overseeing such operation." *Corporate Directors' Guidebook, supra* note 2, at 1603; and "the board cannot . . . conduct day-to-day operations." *The Statement of the Business Roundtable, supra* note 2, at 2098. The ALI concludes that "it is widely understood that the board of a publicly held corporation neither does nor can perform those functions [*i.e.*, manage or direct the management] in the usual sense of those terms." ALI §3.02, Comment at 68 (T.D. No. 2, 1984). Any such effort clearly would be impossible. Conrad, Mace, Blough, Gibson, *Functions of Directors Under the Existing System*, 27 Bus. Law. 23 (1972).

[11] *See, e.g.*, N.Y. Non-Profit Corp. Law, §510(a)(2) (disposition of all the assets to be authorized by directors in a nonmember corporation), §514 (delegation of investment management), §519 (annual report of directors), §602(c) (by-laws may be amended by the board unless otherwise stated in the charter or by-laws), §706 (removal of directors), §714 (removal of officers), §717 (duties of directors), §720(b)(1) (action against directors and officers for misconduct), §721–727 (indemnification), §802(a)(2) (amendment of the certificate of incorporation by the board of a nonmember corporation), §902 (plan of merger or consolidation) or §903 (approval of plan), §1001 (plan of dissolution and distribution of assets) and §1002 (authorization of plan).

Individual directors *qua* directors only possess collective authority and may only exercise power collectively. *Knapp v. Rochester Dog Protective Ass'n.*, 235 App. Div. 436, 257 N.Y.S. 356 (4th Dep't 1932) ("whatever is done must be the deliberate action of the body, and not of its individual members.") *Id.* at 358.

[12] The RMNCA §8.01, Official Comment (Exposure Draft 1986) notes that "the role played by the boards . . . varies widely due to

the nature, size, characteristics and needs of the organizations." This dictates only the most general provisions in enabling boards to accommodate such varying needs.

[13] This weakness in the nonprofit laws derives from the dynamics of the legislative drafting process, the availability of sources and points of reference in the dominant mode of corporate law, and the congeniality of familiar, if not entirely congruent, models. Some effort, however, is being made to address these shortcomings in the RMNCA. *See, e.g.*, RMNCA §8.30, Official Commentary (Exposure Draft 1986).

[14] *John A. Creighton Home for Girls' Trust v. Waltman* 140 Neb. 3, 299 N.W. 261, 268. (1941).

[15] The nonprofit literature devotes considerable attention to the significance of the volunteer board chair and the chair's role within the organization; this is in sharp contrast with the literature of the business corporation, except, of course, where the chair is also the CEO. *See, e.g.*, Clarke, Ference, Hart & Whitehead, *The Role of the Board Chairman or President* (B. W. Mahoney, ed. 1985).

[16] *Cf. Santos v. Chappell*, 318 N.Y.S.2d 570 (1971). Presumably, such a functional analysis would be applied in determining who were *de facto* officers.

Chapter Four

[1] H. Henn & J. Alexander, *Laws of Corporations*, 611 et. seq. (1983).

[2] As part of the dialogue over the ALI corporate governance project, Harvard Law School Professor Victor Brudney, a staunch defender of the project, termed quarrels over "particular phrases" "arid" in light of the paucity of cases holding business directors liable for misconduct. The latter observation, of course, is true *a fortiori* for nonprofit directors. Analysis of the relevant nonprofit cases "suggests that the label given to the standard of care does not determine whether judges . . . will condemn the irresponsible or fraudulent

with the Directors and Trustees of Charitable Organizations, 64 Va.
L. Rev. 449, 465 (1978). But, cf. Fishman, *Standards of Conduct for
Directors of Nonprofit Corporations* 7 Pace Rev. 389 (1987).

[3] *See, e.g.*, Note, *Corporations: Fiduciary Duty*, 24 Cath. U. L. Rev.
656, 656 (1975); *Duties of Charitable Trust Trustees and Charitable
Corporation Directors*, 2 Real Prop. Prob. & Trust J. 545, 545
(1967); Marsh, *Governance of Nonprofit Organizations: An Appropriate Standard of Conduct for Trustees and Directors of Museums
and Other Cultural Institutions*, 65 Dick. L. Rev. 607, 607–08
(1980–81).

[4] Comment, *Trusts—Gifts to Charitable Corporations—Nature of Interest Created—Duties of Trustee*, 26 S. Cal. L. Rev. 80, 83–4
(1952–53).

[5] Bright, *New Investment Management Tools and Strategies* in Non-
Profit Organizations, Current Issues and Development 9, 12 (1984);
Kurtz, *Non-Traditional Revenue Ventures of Tax-Exempt Organizations: The Role of Trustees*, 39 Rec. of the City of N.Y. B. A., 129,
136 (1984); Troyer, Slocombe & Boisture, *Divestment of South Afri-
can Investments: The Legal Implications for Foundations, Other
Charitable Institutions and Pension Funds*, 74 Geo. L.J. 127, 131
(1985).

[6] *See, e.g.*, Ga. Non-Profit Corp. Code §14–3–113; La. Non-Profit
Corp. Law §12:226; Minn. Non-Profit Corp. Act §317.20(6).

[7] *See, e.g.*, Conn. Nonstock Corp. Act §33–447(d); Ohio Non-Profit
Corp. Law §1702.30.

[8] Cal. Non-Profit Public Benefit Corp. Law §5231.

[9] Centner, *Georgia Business and Nonprofit Corporations: Directors'
Duties of Loyalty and Care*, 19 Ga. St. B. J. 164, 165 (1982–83).
Neither the MBCA nor MNCA contained any duty of care provision
until 1974.

[10] *Graham Bros. Co. v. Galloway Woman's College*, 81 S.W. 2d 837,
840 (Ark. 1935); *Beard v. Achenbach Memorial Hospital Associa-*

tion, 170 F.2d 859 (10th Cir. 1948); *Lynch v. John M. Redfield Fdtn.*, 9 Cal. App. 3d 293, 88 Cal. Rptr. 86 (1970) (an exception in that it espouses a trust standard); *Midlantic National Bank v. Frank G. Thompson, etc.*, 170 N.J. Super. 128, 405 A.2d 866 (1979). There are several other equally persuasive expositions of the duty of care, although not where the articulations of the standard is essential to the decision in the case and, thus, could be viewed as *dicta. John A. Creighton Home for Poor Working Girls' Trust v. Waltman,* 140 Neb. 3, 299 N.W. 261 (1941); *George Pepperdine Fdtn. v. Pepperdine,* 126 Cal. App 2d 154, 271 P.2d 600 (1954); *Yarnall Warehouse & Transfer, Inc. v. Three Ivory Bros. Moving Co.*, 226 So.2d 887 (Fla. Dist. Ct. App. 1969).

[11] *Lynch v. Redfield,* 9 Cal. App. 3d 293, 88 Cal. Rptr. 86 (1970).

[12] Although the opinion is somewhat unclear, the uninvested funds appear to have constituted all of the foundation's assets. The court also suggested that the two "innocent" trustees, who unsuccessfully pleaded good faith, might be entitled to indemnity from the third culpable trustee. Cases involving uninvested funds—*e.g., Stern v. Lucy Webb Hayes National Training School for Deaconnesses & Missionaries (The Sibley Hospital Case)*, 381 F.Supp. 1003 (D.C.D.C. 1974) and *Blankenship v. Boyle,* 329 F.Supp. 1089 (D.C.D.C. 1971)—seem to exert a particularly strong pull on the sympathies of courts, manifesting perhaps, a legacy of their trust law antecedents, trustees being under a duty to make the trusts productive.

[13] *Virginia Mason Hospital Assoc. v. Larson,* 114 P.2d 976, 983 (Sup. Ct. Wa. 1941).

[14] *People v. Larkin,* 413 F.Supp. 978 (N.D. Cal. 1976).

[15] RMNCA §8.30, Official Comment (Exposure Draft 1986).

[16] The typical statute simply does not specify in any detail what acts or omissions on the part of directors will be regarded as a dereliction of their duty—even something as obvious, for example, as the necessity of regular attendance at meetings. Clearly, meetings occupy a central position in the architecture of corporate governance. There are, for example, numerous cases that scrutinize what was and

wasn't discussed, whether a quorum was present, or whether other formalities were met. *American Center for Education v. Cavnar* 145 Cal. Rptr. 736, 80 Cal. App.3d 476 (an argument in a bank, in the presence of the bank manager, between three directors of the Center about authority over Center funds was found to be a meeting, albeit an informal one, leading to the ousting of a director). Most of the corporate statutes (nonprofit and business) have extensive provisions concerning the formalities of calling and conducting a meeting. Directors are effectively admonished to participate actively by imposing liability on them for specified unlawful acts if they do not dissent on the record (silence is not golden!). *See, e.g.*, N.Y. Bus. Corp. Law §719(b) and Not-for-Profit Corp. Law §719(b). Yet, nowhere does any statute actually require attendance at meetings, although absence in some circumstances may be equated with assent. Perhaps this is what former Dean Bayless Manning meant when he said that American law does not take the corporation seriously and that, in a wonderful phrase, our corporation statutes are "towering skyscrapers of rusted girders, internally welded together and containing nothing but wind." Manning, *The Stockholders' Appraisal Remedy: An Essay for Frank Coker*, 72 Yale L. J. 223, 245 n. 37 (1962).

Thus, it is impossible to state unequivocally, as obvious as the answer may be, even such an apparent truth as that the duty of care requires regular attendance at board meetings, or, if some level of attendance can be deduced, what the required degree of regularity is. It is clear, from numerous comments, in a number of liability cases, that nonattendance, the subject of critical judicial comment, is a key factor in assessing whether or not directors have performed responsibly. *See also, Stern v. Lucy Webb Hayes* 381 F.Supp. 1003, 1014 (D.C.D.C. 1974) and *Blankenship v. Boyle* 329 F.Supp. 1089, 1102 (D.C.D.C. 1971); *US v. Mt. Vernon Mortgage Corp.* 128 F. Supp 629, 634 (D.C.D.C. 1954); *Eurich & Mathews v. Korean Fdtn., Inc.*, 31 Ill. App. 2d 474, 176 N.E.2d 692, 698 (1961).

[17] ALI, at 26–27 (T.D. No. 3, 1984).

[18] However, the court in *Lynch v. John Redfield*, 9 Cal. App. 3d, at 302, explicity rejected such a good faith defense.

[19] *See, e.g., Ray, v. Homewood Hospital*, 27 N.W.2d 409, 411 (Minn. 1947).

[20] A ban on employee directors may deprive volunteer directors from relying on those with more information and expertise. For a further discussion of the membership of nonprofit boards, see chapter Two, notes 9–11, and accompanying text.

[21] ALI §4.02, Comment (T.D. No. 4, 1985).

[22] In performing their functions consistently with the duty of care, directors may rely on board committees and certain experts both for information ("reliance") and action ("delegation"). Although the comprehensive RMNCA formulation (*See* RMNCA §8.30, Official Comment [Exposure Draft 1986]) explicitly covers the scope of permitted reliance on corporate officers and experts as well as delegation to committees, not all statutes are so explicit or extensive. In fact, comparable reliance or delegation in some jurisdictions would seem not to be permitted. Although this is inconsistent with sound policy and actual practice in most cases, the slowness of legal developments in the nonprofit area is troubling in defining potential liabilities. *See also*, N.Y. Not-for-Profit Corp. Law §717.

[23] These vary somewhat from state to state, although for organizations without members—the great majority—there are few nondelegable functions. Typically, such nondelegable matters include authorizing fundamental corporate changes, adopting by-law amendments, modifying members' rights, fixing the compensation of directors, etc. *See, e.g.*, N.Y. Not-for-Profit Corp. Law §712(a); Del. Bus. Corp. Law §141(c).

[24] ALI Intro Note, at 2–3 (T.D. No. 4, 1985).

[25] The confusion in this area over the applicability of principles of trust law and corporate law is pervasive. There is little question, for example, that the directors of corporations must extensively delegate their duties and that such delegations are well recognized. In the language of business management literature, the "span of control" otherwise would limit drastically the size and complexity of any corporate enterprise were directors actually required to "manage" an organization without substantial delegation.

Trustees, at least at common law, could not do so and most

certainly could not delegate their investment responsibilities. This nondelegation rule was carried over into the view of charitable directors' responsibilities. The promulgation of UMIFA and its adoption in twenty-nine states reflects the general concern about these perceived limitations. *See Midlantic Nat. Bank v. Frank G. Thompson, etc.* 170 N.J.Super. 128, 405 A.2d 866 (1979); W. Cary & C. Bright, *The Developing Law of Endowment Funds: The Law and the Lore Revisited*, 21 et seq. Obviously, the widespread need to adopt such legislation reflects the great unease about the propriety of otherwise permitting delegation. At the same time, there are few today who could argue convincingly, even in a trust context, that delegation is not acceptable and may, perhaps, be obligatory in some situations. A significant remaining difference between trustees—private or charitable—and charitable directors, is that the former are personally compensated, often handsomely, and the latter typically serve gratuitously and, even when compensated, as in the case of private foundation directors, receive only modest payment. Thus, requiring trustees to labor personally for their rewards makes some sense while compelling unpaid directors to do so and, at the same time, expect able service is illusory. *See* N.Y. Surr. Ct. Proc. Act §2309 (establishes compensation of trustees as a declining percentage of assets managed).

Courts have recognized "that those who give of their time for the public good by serving on boards of charitable corporations need assistance to meet . . . requirements [of the position] . . ." *Midlantic Nat. Bank,* 405 A.2d 866, at 871 (N.J. Super. Ch. 1979). That granted, the extent of the need for such services and the cost are business judgments for directors to make so long as the costs remain reasonable. The formulation of the business judgment rule, of course, assumes that there is no conflicting interest present and that there is a rational (or reasonable) basis for the judgment.

[26] New York's BCL permits board members to make extensive delegations in keeping with current corporate practice. While the omission of comparable reliance provisions from the N-PCL might be regarded as an oversight, principles of statutory construction could mitigate against such a conclusion, especially in view of the UMIFA provisions on broad investment delegation and their exculpation of directors who properly exercise such delegation authority. N.Y.

Not-for-Profit Corp. Law §717 permits investment delegation under §512–14, derived from UMIFA §5. The RMNCA has similar provisions.

[27] Cal. Corp. Code 5231(b). *See also* Basile, *Director's Corporate Liability Under the New California Nonprofit Corporate Law*, 13 Univ. of S.F. L. Rev. 891 (1979). UMIFA §6 requires similar due care in the selection of investment delegates.

[28] RMNCA §8.30, Official Comment, in explicating the basic rule of conduct, notes that "under similar circumstances" relates not only to the circumstances of the corporation, but to those of the directors as well—qualifications, background, and experience—and recognizes explicitly that "[m]any directors are elected to the board to raise money or because of financial contributions they have made." However, while they may possess no special skill or background helpful to the corporation, they remain "obligated to act as directors and may not simply act as figureheads." Their fund-raising role, however, should be considered in determining whether they have met their obligations under the prescribed standard.

[29] *See e.g., Graham Bros. Co. v. Galloway Woman's College*, 81 S.W.2d 837, 840 (Sup. Ct. Ark. 1935); *Creighton Home for Girls' Trust v. Waltman*, 299 N.W. 261, 268 (Sup. Ct. Neb. 1941); *Midlantic Nat. Bank*, 170 N.J.Super. 128, at 405 A.2d 866, 871–72 (1979).

[30] Many boards, of course, do this through the creation of honorary or emeritus directors, advisory boards and other vehicles for enhanced giving.

[31] However, if the Executive Director is not regarded as an officer (a determination of his status involves an analysis of the functions the Executive Director performs), under accepted legal principles he would have less extensive liability as an employee.

[32] Where courts take such past generosity into account typically is in deciding what an appropriate penalty might be. *Stern v. Lucy Webb Hayes National Training School* 367 F. Supp. 536 (D.D.C. 1973).

[33] Again, as already noted, most statutes require a director receiving an advance to promise in writing to repay it, although the promise need not be secured in any way. *See* ch. Six, notes 26–28 and accompanying text for a further discussion of this topic.

[34] At the same time, it should be noted, with some care, that insurance would not cover expenses incidental to an investigation that did not mature into a lawsuit. *See generally*, Lazar, *Form and Structure of Defense & Settlement Clauses in Directors's & Officers Policies*, in D&O Liability Insurance and Self-Insurance, 235 (PLI 1986).

[35] The board also benefits from its own internal dynamics where Board members may depend on the proven wisdom or judgment of fellow directors.

[36] Most statutes permit committees to exercise broad delegated authority except for a few specific actions (such as changing the by-laws, filling board vacancies, fixing director compensation, approving fundamental transactions: merger, sales, etc.). *See* N.Y. N-PCL §712. For a further discussion of the business judgment rule, see notes 0–53 and accompanying text.

[37] One area to guard against in such a situation would be potential conflicts or self-dealing arising from actual or potential relationships between members of the same profession. For example, the Development Director might have some interest in future employment with the professional consultant, which could color her actions, not necessarily intentionally. This is an issue to which a committee or board must be attuned.

[38] Most directors tend not to be adversarial about these matters and the dynamics of board meetings are most often consensual. *See, e.g.* Manning, *The Business Judgment Rule and the Director's Duty of Attention: Time for Reality* 39 Bus. Law. 1477 (1984); Middleton, *The Place and Power of Non-Profit Boards of Directors* (PONPO Working Paper No. 78, 1983).

[39] Information gathering and evaluating has a cost calculus that must be kept in mind in deciding how much information is needed for a decision.

[40] After grappling with the content of the rule and its relation to the duty of care for five years, the ABA's Committee on Corporate Law, guardian of the Revised Model Business Corporation Act, simply gave up the effort to reach a definitive construction of the business judgment rule, concluding that because "the elements of the . . . rule and the circumstances for its application are continuing to be developed," codification of the rule is "a task left to the courts and . . . later revisions of this Model Act." RMBCA §8.30, Official Comment (1984). Thus, confident statements of its applicability to nonprofit organizations seem misplaced.

[41] Id. at §4.01(c)(1),(2), and (3).

[42] Fischel, *The Business Judgment Rule and the Trans Union Case*, 40 Bus. Law. 1437 (1985); Manning, *supra*, note 38.

[43] Professor Fischel, in suggesting that the decision to acquire information or not itself be shielded from scrutiny, emphasizes the superior incentives and capacity of managers to reach "optimum" results. While the simplicity of the economic objective may make this appropriate in a business context, it is doubtful that the diffuse nature of the nonprofit mission can provide similar assurances. Nonprofit managers, of course, have no such incentives and there are no large shareholders to affect policy—only a somewhat nebulous general public interest. Fischel, *supra* note 42, at 1441–43. In any case, the "discipline of the capital markets" is unavailing in a nonprofit context. Kurtz, *supra* note 5, at 133.

[44] Abrams, *Regulating Charity: The State's Role*, 35 Rec. of the City of N.Y.B.A. 481, 486 (1980).

[45] *Graham Bros. v. Galloway*, 81 S.W.2d 837 (Ark. 1935) ("the members of the . . . committee were men of business ability and their honesty of purpose is not questioned"); *Creighton v. Waltman*, 140 Neb. 3, 299 N.W. 261 (1941) ("a proper exercise of the business judgment of the trustee, controlled by the honesty and integrity of the men who manage the trust"); *Beard v. Achenbach*, 170 F.2d 859 (10th Cir. 1948) ("directors . . . acting in good faith and within the limitations of the law have the power to determine its policies and manage its affairs"); *Yarnall v. Three Ivory Bros.*, 226 So.2d 887

(Fla. App. 1969) ("the lower court was correct in not substituting its judgment . . . absent a clear showing of bad faith . . . or abuse of business judgment"). However, *Yarnall* appears to be a misapplication of the rule, involving, as it did, a conflicting interest. *See, also, Edson v. Griffin Hospital*, 21 Conn. Sup. 55, 144 A. 2d 341 (1958) ("questions of policy and management are left solely to the honest decisions of the officers and directors"). A recent case, *Morris v. Scribner*, 69 N.Y. 2d 418, 508 N.E. 2d 136, 515 N.Y.S. 2d 424 1987), seems to endorse an expansive application of the business judgment rule to religious corporations. It is unclear whether such deference to private decision making is constitutionally based.

This is a conceptual difference that has plagued the courts continually in attempting to define the rule itself. *See, e.g., Smith v. Van Gorkom*, 488 A.2d 858 (Del. Sup. Ct. 1985). There would appear to be little practical difference between application of a "gross negligence" standard as in *Parish v. Virginia Milk*, 261 Md. 618, 277 A.2d 19 or a "business judgment rule" as in *Beard v. Achenbach*.

[46] *See* ALI §4.01(c), Comment (T.D. No. 4, 1985); RMNCA §8.30, Official Comment (3) at 856–57 (Exposure Draft 1986).

[47] Courts implicitly or explicity reflect this. *See, e.g. Cross v. Midtown Club, Inc.*, 33 Conn. Sup. 150, 365 A.2d 1227 (1976), in which the court, although finding defendants had unlawfully excluded women from a social club, permitted the award to defendants of the expenses of their unsuccessful defense ("Given the fact . . . that the *unpaid* directors . . . were simply following . . . the existing policy of the club") [emphasis supplied)] *Id.* at 1231–32. *But c.f., Lynch v. Redfield, supra,* note 18 (unquestioning subjective good faith does not exculpate directors for the negligence of fellow directors).

[48] *See, e.g.* Simon, *Charity and Dynasty Under the Federal Tax System*, 5 Prob. Law. 1 (1978); RMNCA §8–30 (Exposure Draft 1986); *In the Matter of Multiple Sclerosis Service Organization of New York,* Inc. 68 N.Y. 2d 32, 496 N.E. 2d 861, 505 N.Y.S. 2d 841, at 848 (1986). supra, n. 94 at 848.

[49] *Parish v. Virginia Milk* 277 A.2d at 48 (Md. 1971); *Beard v. Achenbach*, 170 F.2d at 862 (10th Cir. 1948).

[50] This example is derived from a case study of a Wells College plan described in M. Keil & J. Crimmins, *Enterprise in the Nonprofit Sector*, 48–49, (1983).

[51] ALI, at 58 (T.D. No. 4, 1985).

[52] *Id.*

[53] *Treadway Companies, Inc. v. Care Corp.*, 638 F.2d 357, 382 (2d Cir. 1980); *Lewis v. S.L.E. , Inc.* 629 F.2d 764, 769 (2d Cir. 1980); *Bayer v. Beran*, 49 N.Y.S.2d 2, at 6–11 (Sup. Ct. N.Y. Co. 1944).

[54] *See generally*, ALI §5.11 (T.D. No. 3, 1984).

[55] In *Societa Operaia Di Mutuo Soccorso Villalba v. DiMaria*, 40 N.J. Supp. 344, 122 A.2d 897 (1956), the court found a violation of the duty of loyalty in the treasurer's failure to collect income from a social club's leesee, who was related to him by marriage. "[A] trustee can be disloyal . . . just as significantly by seeking the advantage of a third person as by looking to his own private aggrandizement." *Id.* at 899.

[56] *See, e.g., Brown v. Memorial National Home Foundation*, 162 Cal. App. 2d 513, 329 P.2d 118 (1958) (assumption of an adverse charitable trust is grounds for removal).

[57] IRC §501(c)(3); IRS Reg. §1.501(c)(3)–1(d)(1)(ii); *See, e.g., Texas Trade School*, 30 TC 642, Dec. 23,040, *aff'd per curiam*, CA–5, 59–2 USTC & 9786, 272 F.2d 168; *Gemological Institute of America, Inc.*, 17 TC 1604, Dec. 18,868, *aff'd per curiam*, CA–9, 54–1 USTC & 9339, 212 F.2d 205; *Gemological Institute of America, Inc.*, DC, 57–1 UWTC & 9418, 149 F.Supp. 128; *Birmingham Business College, Inc.*, CA–5, 60–1 USTC & 9371, 276 F.2d 476.

[58] *See, e.g.*, N.Y. Not-for Profit Corp. Law §§102(a)(5), 204, 508, 515, 516; *Kubik v. American Composers Alliance*, 54 N.Y.S. 2d 764 (1965); *Bennet v. American-Canadian Ambulance Corp.*, 179 Misc. 21, 37 N.Y.S. 2d 470 (1942).

[59] ALI Part V (T.D. No. 3, 1984) *passim*; RMBCA §8.31, Official Commentary (1984).

[60] *See, e.g.*, Del. Gen. Corp. Law §143; N.Y. Not-for-Profit Corp. Law §716.

[61] RMBCA §8.31, Official Comment at 227–28 (1984).

[62] *Fowle Memorial Hospital Co. v. Nicholson*, 189 N.C. 44, 126 S.E. 94 (1925); *Samuel and Jessie Kenney Presbyterian Home v. State*, 24 P.2d 403 (Sup. Ct. Wa. 1933); *Gilbert v. McLeod Infirmary*, 219 S.C. 174, 64 S.E.2d 524 (1951); *Mount Vernon*, 128 F.Supp. 629; *Blankenship v. Boyle*, 329 F.Supp. 1089; *Mountain Top Youth Camp, Inc. v. Lyon*, 20 N.C.App. 694, 202 S.E.2d 498 (1974).

[63] ALI §5.02, Comment (T.D. No. 5, 1986) (cases cited at p. 48). *See also*, RMBCA, §8.31, Official Commentary (1984).

While §8.30 of the RMNCA purports to encapsulate a general duty of loyalty by requiring directors' action to be "in the best interests" of the corporation, there does not appear to be any support for this position in the RMBCA, upon which the RMNCA was modeled. In any event, the "best interests" language does not necessarily exclude action that, at least in part, is *self-interested*, the key to compliance with the duty.

[64] *See, e.g.*, N.Y. Not-for-Profit Corp. Law §715; Del. Gen. Corp. Law §144; Cal. Corp. Code §5233(d)(1)–(3).

[65] In some instances, committees or agencies of the state may scrutinize such a transaction. *See e.g.*, Cal. Corp. Code §5233(3)(c); RMNCA §8.31 (Exposure Draft 1986).

[66] This suggests that there must be a minimum of two or three directors. ALI §5.04, Comment (T.D. No. 3, 1984); N.Y. Not-For-Profit Corp. Law §§702(a), 707, 715; RMBCA, §8.31(c) (1984); *but c.f.*, Del. Gen. Corp. Law §144(b) which allows single member boards.

[67] The RMNCA makes the belief by noninterested directors in the transaction's fairness an element required for advance approval. RMNCA §8.31(b)(1)(ii) (Exposure Draft 1986).

[68] It should be noted that for conflicts purposes, "fairness" is not a single number, *i.e.*, the best price obtainable, but represents a

"range of reasonableness" within which conflicts transactions are to be sustained. ALI. §5.08(a)(2)(A), Comment at 119 (T.D. No. 3, 1984); c.f., *Matter of Horticultural Society of New York, Inc.*, N.Y.L.J. April 1st, 1980, at 5, col. 1M.

[69] *Fowle Memorial*, 189 N.C. 44, 126 S.E. 94, 97 (1925).

[70] *Gilbert v. McLeod Infirmary*, 64 S.E.2d 524, 529 (S.C. 1951).

[71] *See, e.g., Mt. Vernon Mortgage Corp.*, 128 F. Supp. at 636 (sale of organization's sole asset set aside when action of trustees was wholly uninformed, resulting in disposition of asset for a fraction of its value) and *Bolton v. Stillwagon*, 410 Pa. 618, 190 A.2d 105 (failure of directors to disclose self-dealing inconsistent with assertion of good faith and results in rescission).

[72] As the Commentary to the RMBCA makes clear, "[t]he elimination of the automatic rule of voidability does not mean that all transactions that meet one or more of the [statute's] test . . . are automatically valid. These transactions may be subject to attack on a variety of grounds . . . for example, that the transactions constituted waste." RMBCA §8.31 (1984).

[73] *Fowle Memorial*, 189 N.C. 44, 126 S.E. 94 (lease of hospital to directors); *Knapp v. Rochester Dog Protective Association*, 235 App. Div. 436, 257 N.Y.S. 356 (4th Dept't 1932) (rental payments to director for use of property "donated" to organization); *McLeod Infirmary*, 64 S.E.2d 524 (S.C. 1951) (attempted sale of hospital property to trustees); *Mt. Vernon Mortgage Corp*, 128 F. Supp. 629 (D.D.C. 1954) (transfer of building company shares representing corporation's sole asset to corporation controlled by certain trustees); and *Mountain Top*, 20 N.C.App. 694, 202 S.E.2d 498 (1974) (transfer of camp property to former director and officer).

[74] *Old Settlers Club of Milwaukee County v. Haun*, 245 Wis. 213, 13 N.W.2d 913 (1944) (securities transactions through director's brokerage business); *Korean Fdtn. Inc.* 31 Ill. App. 2d 474, 176 N.E.2d 692, 699 (investment of corporate funds in directors' businesses); *Stern*, 381 F. Supp. 1003 (nonproductive deposit of hospital funds in banks of which directors were officers/directors); *People v.*

Larkin, 413 F. Supp. 978 (D.C.N.D. Cal. 1976) (use of foundation funds to secure loan to business of foundation director).

The *Stern ("Sibley Hospital")* case really deserves its own footnote. In many ways, what is most remarkable about this renowned case is its unremarkability. Part of this case can be understood against the case's peculiar history and Judge Gesell's own experience. The Sibley case was commenced within two years of Judge Gesell's decision in *Blankenship v. Boyle*, 329 F.Supp. 1089, a case involving the mismanagement of millions of dollars of United Mine Workers welfare funds. The principal failing by the trustees in that case was their toleration of huge sums of uninvested cash. Thus, it may be assumed, although not proven, that a similar occurrence in the Sibley matter had a peculiar resonance for Judge Gesell; it is the first issue he focuses on in his discussion. However, the duty to maximize the productivity of funds is not nearly so clear as the *Sibley* opinion suggests. By way of contrast, a Florida court has determined, at least in one recent case involving part of the DuPont benefactions, that a 3 percent return satisfactorily fulfills the duty to make funds productive. *State of Delaware, et al. v. J.C. Belin, et al.* No. AS-1199, AS-225, slip op. (Dist. Ct. App., 1st Dist. Fla. 1984). In *Sibley*, the court seems to believe that the self-dealing there (banking relations and securities transactions with firms owned or controlled by hospital board members) was less culpable because most of those relationships were initiated by hospital officers. That, of course, is precisely the way real conflicts problems present themselves. The trustees themselves, who have the conflicts, need to be consulted about such matters and they, undoubtedly, are only too well aware, if not of the hospital's manifold activities, then of the activities and interests of their own firms. To nonprofit senior staff and officers, to whom trustees are understandably potent figures, the human desire to propitiate the powerful, may lead precisely to such untoward results. The potential for establishing such conflict relationships is simply too tempting—if not for the trustees, then for a dependant staff eager to please. In fact, the *Sibley* court itself recognizes the value of prevention: "[t]he best way to avoid potential conflicts of interest and to be assured of objective advice is to avoid the possibility of such conflicts at the time . . . trustees are selected." *Id.* at 1019. There are other ironies in Sibley as well. Although finding that "the handling of hospital funds rests equally on all Board members," it notes that the defendants are "but a small miniority of the full . . . Board." Yet, despite the law's imposition of a duty of care of equal force on all directors, virtually no step is taken to assure the active functioning of the board except for the adoption of various investment policies, disclosure of conflicts, and some "jawboning."

[75] *Societa Operaia DiMutuo Soccorso Villalba v. DiMaria*, 40 N.J. Super. 344, 122 A.2d 897 (1956) (officer failed to collect income from rental property due to a personal relationship with the lessee); *Brown v. Memorial National Home Foundation*, 329 P.2d 118 (Cal. App. 1958) (diversion by an officer of corporate property for the benefit of separate charitable organization controlled by the same officer); *Blankenship*, 329 F. Supp. 1089 (use of unproductive funds by banks controlled by union of which Fund's directors were officers).

[76] *Bolton v. Stillwagon*, 410 Pa. 618, 190 A.2d 105 (1963) (purchase of corporate investment at foreclosure sale by directors); *Mile-O-Mo Fishing Club v. Noble*, 62 Ill. App. 2d 50, 210 N.E.2d 12 (1965) (purchase of corporate property by president for personal use); *Valle v. North Jersey Automobile Club*, 125 N.J. Super. 302, 210 A.2d 518 (1973); *aff'd as modified*, 141 N.J. Super. 568, 359 A.2d 504 (1976); *aff'd as modified*, 74 N.J. 109, 376 A.2d 1192 (club's directors acquired for their own interest an insurance agency serving club's members).

[77] *Virginia Mason*, 114 P.2d 976 (S. Ct. Wa. 1941); *Beard v. Achenbach*, 170 F.2d 859 (10th Cir. 1948).

[78] *See, e.g., Bolton*, 410 Pa. 618, 190 A.2d 105.

[79] Many major institutions have lawyers, bankers, or others on their boards whose services are obtained on a favorable basis. While this may be inevitable in some cases and, perhaps, even desirable, it is instructive to note, by way of contrast, the declining representation of, for example, outside counsel on business boards.

[80] While conflicts issues generate enormous interest among lawyers and command much of the public's attention because of the potential

drama and, occasionally, lurid scenarios, any discussion of them should be placed in proper context. For the vast majority of non-profit organizations, conflicts issues simply do not arise frequently, at least not in the direct way contemplated by the legal framework intended to deal with such situations. A lawyer/director of several well-known major nonprofit institutions has told me that in all her years of service, a conflicts issue had never surfaced at the board level. Despite what lawyers familiar with governance issues may think, directors' responsibilities leave scant time in their agendas for the niceties of standards of care and conflicts. Their primary task is to run an organization. In an illuminating report on the demanding business life of the chief executive officer of a major American corporation, there is not a single reference to, or discussion of, any of these aspects of governance, although board relations are mentioned, albeit briefly. Kleinfield, *What It Takes: The Life of a C.E.O.*, The N.Y. Times Magazine, Dec. 1, 1985, at 32. *But cf.*, Opinion Research Corp. and Research Strategies Corp., Directors' and Officers' Liability: A Crisis in the Making 11 (Peat, Marwick, Mitchell, Co. 1987).

[81] The conflicts provisions that today are the prevalent standard are virtually identical to those pertaining to business corporations. Perhaps one explanation of their generally modest level of protection is their derivation from a context in which the profit-motive is pervasive and, presumably, the morals of the marketplace the norm. Thus, fellow directors may be presumed to be on their guard.

[82] *Compare, e.g., Gilbert v. McLeod* 64 S.E.2d 524 (S.C. 1951), with *Ivory Bros. v. Yarnall*, 226 So.2d 887 (Fla. 1969). In the former case, the court correctly found a prohibited conflict even though the participation of the interested directors and a non-director ally were not needed either for a quorum or approval. The court perceptively noted that "[t]he influence of the interested director is not measured by his vote alone, but his participation in the meeting, his arguments and the weight of his judgment . . ." *Gilbert* at 530. On the other hand, in *Yarnall* the court permitted a challenged transaction, although an interested director, one of eighteen, had both voted and spoken in favor of rejecting a competitor's application. *Yarnall*, at 892.

[83] Cal. Corp. Code §5233(d)(2)(D) and §9243(d)(3)(3). *The Corporate Director's Guidebook* notes that a commonly used standard involves "ascertainment that the proposed transaction is on at least as favorable terms to the corporation as might be available . . . from any other person or entity." 33 Bus. Law. 1591, 1599 (1978). The RMBCA defines fairness as being "within the range that might have been entered into at arm's length by disinterested persons." RMBCA §8.31, Official Comment at 4 (1984).

[84] *See, generally*, IRC §4941 and IRC Reg. §53.4941 *et seq.*

[85] Kurtz, *supra* note 5, at 132 (1984).

[86] McGovern, *The Changing Character of Exempt Organizations*, The Philanthropy Monthly, April 1986, at 19.

[87] *See, e.g., Aliberti v. Green*, 6 Mass.App. 41, 372 N.E.2d 534 (1978). *But c.f., Collins v. Beinecke*, 67 N.Y. 2d 479, 495, N.E.2d 335, 504 N.Y.S.2d 72 (1986) (directors of a corporate foundation owed their primary loyalty to the foundation they served and not to the corporation whose benefactions sustained the foundation); *Raven's Cove Townhouses, Inc. v. Knuppe Dev.* 114 Cal. App. 3d 783, 171 Cal. Rptr. 334 (1981) (condominium association's directors who served as nominees of developer during organizational stage owed no lesser duty of loyalty to association members' interests).

[88] *See, e.g., Milton Frank Allen Publications, Inc. v. Georgia Association of Petroleum Retailers, Inc.*, 224 Ga. 518, 162 S.E.2d 724 (1968), *cert. denied*, 339 U.S. 1025 (critical board functions may not be delegated to others).

[89] The RMNCA continues this prohibition. *See* RMNCA, §8.32 (Exposure Draft 1986).

[90] Cal. Not-for-Profit Corp. Law §5236.

[91] N.Y. Educ. Law. §216(a)(4)(a)(8). Institutions of higher learning traditionally have assisted employees, including officers (e.g., the president) with housing needs and/or actually provided housing.

[92] Of course, the IRS also might scrutinize such arrangements as potential circumventions of the nondistribution constraint.

[93] The other directors might incur liability on either of two premises: they knew and, out of a misguided loyalty to an individual, failed to act, or they did not know because of poor internal controls or monitoring devices, but breached their duty of care by not knowing.

[94] ALI, 161 (T.D. No. 3, 1984).

[95] ALI, §§5.08 (c), 5.09(c), 5.11(c) and 5.12(d) (T.D. No 3, 1984).

[96] It is worth noting that the ALI Project would disqualify certain former officers from filling "independent" slots on, for example, audit committees because they are involved in relationships that may impair their objectivity, in passing on the assessments of their own past actions as officers, their mentor relationships with current officers and their continuing receipt of corporate payments being conditional on, e.g., noncompetition clauses enforceable at the discretion of current officers. ALI, §3.03 (T.D. No. 2, 1984).

[97] As with former officers, the ALI proposals would disqualify general counsel from the exercise of certain responsibilities requiring independence. Under a number of state indemnification statutes, the exercise of independent judgment is frequently called for by special or independent legal counsel who, presumably, is not the same as the general counsel. N.Y. Not-for-Profit Corp. §§724(b)(2)(a).

[98] Under the Internal Revenue Code's self-dealing provisions, foundation managers (this includes officers and directors) could not be part of a group of employees or managers purchasing foundation assets without subjecting themselves or the foundation to prohibitive penalties. Treas. Reg. §53.4941(d)-2(f), T.D.7983, 1984-1 C.B. 212. In this example, however, if the "excess" business holdings of the foundation were acquired prior to the adoption in 1969 of these rules, the transaction effecting compliance with the excess business holdings rules would be exempt from self-dealing penalties. Treas. Reg. §21.53.4941(d)-4(b), T.D. 7678, 1980-1 C.B. 255. In any case, self-dealing could be cured if the two officers ceased to be

"disqualified persons," which they could do simply by resigning their positions with the foundation prior to the consummation of any such transaction. I.R.C. §4946(b)(1); Treas. Reg §53.4946–1(f)(1)(i).

[99] The related *ultra vires* doctrine, while virtually moribund in the context of business corporations, retains surprising vitality in the nonprofit area where the doctrine is still imbued with its trust law origins and reflects an enduring reality. *See* Moody, *Nonprofit Corporations: A Survey of Recent Cases*, 21 Clev. St. L. Rev. 26, 39–40 (1972); Note, *Dissolution of Public Charity Corporations: Preventing Improper Distribution of Assets*, 50 Tex. L. Rev. 1429, 1434 (1981).

[100] *Commonwealth of Pennsylvania v. Barnes Foundation*, 398 Pa. 158, 159 A.2d 500, 505 (1960) (though trust language is employed, the case involved a charitable corporation organized under a will).

[101] Report of the Committee on Charitable Trusts, Thomas Eubank, Chairman, *Duties of Charitable Trust Trustees and Charitable Corporation Directors*, 2 Real Prop. Prob. and Tr. J. 545 (1967); A. W. Scott, II *Scott on Trusts* §§164, 164(1), 169 (1967).

[102] *Trustees of Rutgers College in New Jersey v. Grover C. Richman Jr.*, 41 N.J. Super. 259, 125 A.2d 10, 26 (1956).

[103] Runquist, *Responsibilities and Duties of a Director of a Nonprofit Organization*, Charitable Giving §§509, 509.1 (Prentice Hall, 1985); *Brown v. Memorial National Home Fdtn.*, 329 P.2d 118 (Cal. App. 1958) (diversion of charitable funds to unauthorized purposes, even if charitable, is grounds for removal of the chief executive).

[104] An organization's purposes may be defined by what it does as well as what it says it does. *See, e.g., Queen of Angels Hospital v. Younger*, 136 Cal. Rptr. 36, 66 Cal. App. 3d 359 (1977); *Miami Retreat Foundation v. Ervin*, 62 So.2d 748, 750 (Fla. 1952); *In the Matter of Multiple Sclerosis Service Organization of New York, Inc.*, 68 N.Y.2d 32, 496 N.E.2d 861, 505 N.Y.S.2d 841 (1986).

[105] *See, e.g.,* J. Crimmins and M. Keil, *Enterprise in the Nonprofit Sector* 32 (1983); MacMillan, *Competitive Strategies for Not-for-Profit Agencies,* in I Advances in Strategic Management 61, 62–64 (1983); Better Business Bureau, *Standards for Charitable Solicitations,* Rules I(d), II(a) (1979).

[106] Kurtz, *Hospital Reorganization: Corporate and Policy Implications,* 56 N.Y. St. B. J. 22, 24 (1984); P. Starr, *The Social Transformation of American Medicine* 430–36 (1980).

[107] This explains the unusual persistence of the *ultra vires* doctrine, long moribund in its application to business corporations, as a check on the ability of directors to divert charitable resources to purposes other than those for which they were intended. At one time, of course, when corporations were relative novelties, they, too, were organized for highly specific purposes. G. S. Seward & J. C. Nauss, Jr. *Basic Corporate Practice* xiii (2nd ed. 1977). Indeed, it is difficult to formulate a justification for retention of the *ultra vires* concept in a business context where, after all, there is only a single objective into which a multitude of activities may be translated, *i.e.,* corporate profit and shareholder gain. ALI §2.01 (T.D. No. 2,1983). At the same time, it is impossible to assimilate the multifarious activities pursued by charities to a single objective.

[108] *Alco Gravure v. The Knapp Foundation,* 64 N.Y.2d 458, 479 N.E.2d 752, 490 N.Y.S. 2d 116 (the decision, while abjuring fidelity to charter purposes, leaves open the issue of whether or not the pursuit of a previously unfulfilled charter purpose can be *ultra vires* and, thus, unlawful, without court approval. *See also, Multiple Sclerosis,* 68 N.Y.2d 32, 496 N.E.2d 861, 505 N.Y.S.2d 841 (1986). In this case, the Court of Appeals ruled that under N.Y. Not-for-Profit-Corp. Law §1005(a)(3)(a) the criterion governing the distribution of the assets of a dissolving nonprofit to another nonprofit was whether it was "engaged in activities substantially similar to those of the dissolved corporation." *Id* at 847. Under the common law, the rule was phrased in terms of the original purpose of the testator.

[109] Thus, for example, a hospital's trustees could agree that the management of a hospital may be assumed by another institution,

Holden Hospital Corporation v. Southern Illinois Hospital Corporation, 22 Ill. 2d 150, 174 N.E.2d 793, 798 (1961), or that an institution might be relocated where its charter authorized such a change, *City of Paterson v. The Paterson General Hospital*, 97 N.J. Super. 514, 235 A.2d 487 (1967). An organization is "only under a duty not to divert property to anything other than one or more of the . . . purposes for which the corporation is organized," *Denckla v. Independence Foundation*, 193 A.2d 538, 541 (Del. Supr. 1963), and the board may have very broad discretion in determining how best to do that. *But cf., Attn. Gen. v. Hahnemann Hospital* 397 Mass. 843, 494 N.E.2d 1011 (1986) ("those who give to a home for abandoned animals do not anticipate a future board amending the charity's purpose to become research vivisectionists") *Id.* at 1021. *See also, Multiple Sclerosis Society* 68 N.Y.2d 32, 496 N.E.2d 861, 505 N.Y.S.2d 841 (1986) (in determining whether to grant approval of a proposed distribution of charitable funds in a dissolution, a court should consider (1) the source of the funds, whether received through public subscription or under a will, (2) the stated purposes of the organization, (3) the activities and services provided by it, (4) the activities and purposes of proposed distributees, and (5) the bases for the distribution recommended by the board.

[110] In 1985, individuals contributed more than $66 billion to charitable organizations, a still healthy share of their total support. American Assoc. of Fund-Raising Counsel, *Giving USA: Estimates of Philanthropic Giving in 1985 and the Trends They Show* 2 (1986).

[111] This notion is expressed in a number of cases dealing with changes in organizational purposes. *See, e.g. Multiple Sclerosis Society* 68 N.Y.2d 32, 496 N.E.2d 861, 505 N.Y.S.2d 841 and *Rutgers College* 41 N.J. Super. 259, 125 A.2d 10. This reality is overlooked by those who, like Professor Hansmann, would eliminate the limitations on nonprofit purposes while retaining the nondistribution constraint as the single distinctive characteristic. Hansmann, *Reforming Nonprofit Corporation Law*, 129 U. of Pa. L. Rev. 500, 580 (1981); RMNCA §§3.01 and 3.04 (Exposure Draft 1986). *See, also* Abrams, *Indian Museum Leaders Seem Determined to Leave New York*, N.Y. Times, July 7, 1987, Editorial Page, col. 3 (letter from The New York Attorney General stating "philanthropic

citizens . . . have the right to rely upon the state to insure that their gifts are managed in accordance with their intentions").

[112] This is the only aspect of the duty of obedience that remains viable for business corporations. ALI §2.01(a) (T.D. No. 2, 1984) ([A business corporation] . . . is obliged . . . to act within the boundaries set by law.). Similarly, the *Corporate Director's Guidebook* 33 The Bus. Law. 1595, 1610 (1978), suggests that individual directors be "concerned . . . that the corporation has programs looking toward compliance with applicable laws" and *The Statement of the Business Roundtable* 33 The Bus. Law. 2083, 2101 (1978) largely concurs. Such law compliance obligation, part of the duty of obedience, can equally affect the directors of nonprofit organizations and if such obligations are violated, they also will incur liability. *Tillman v. Wheaton Haven Recreation Association, Inc.*, 517 F.2d 1141 (4th Cir. 1975) (individual directors of community swimming pool held liable for civil rights violation in excluding blacks); *Endress v. Brookdale Community College*, 144 N.J. Super. 109, 364 A.2d 1080 (1976) (officer individually liable for dismissal of faculty advisor to student newspaper arising from violation of her exercise of First Amendment rights). While each of these cases sent shock waves throughout the nonprofit community, the significance is much less far-reaching and certainly less extensive than feared. In both cases, consistent with the general notions of law compliance, directors and officers were deemed to be aware of, and have an appreciation for, well-settled constitutional rights. This, of course, is quite distinct from holding directors and officers liable for technical violations of complex or obscure regulatory schemes, *The Statement of the Business Roundtable, supra*, at 2101.

[113] The Internal Revenue Service has held that a volunteer board is not necessarily exempt from liability for unpaid taxes if certain factors are present in the violation. Rev. Rule 84–83, I.R.B. 1984–24,13; CCH Exempt Organizations Reporter ¶6869. *See also, Hildebrand, Jr. v. U.S.*, 563 F.Supp. 1259 (denial of motion by directors seeking summary dismissal of IRS suit to enforce personal liability of directors of a neighborhood health centre). *See also, Schwinger v. United States* 652 F. Supp. 464 (E.D.N.Y. 1987). *But c.f., Simpson v. United States*, 664 F.Supp. 43 (E.D.N.Y. 1987) (hospital trustee not a "responsible person" under IRC unless "active" in tax matters).

[114] *See, e.g., Corporate Director's Guidebook*, 33 Bus. Law. 1591, 1610 (1978); ALI §2.01 (T.D. No. 2, 1984).

Chapter Five

[1] In the for-profit area, the derivative action has been "the chief regulator of corporate conduct." *Cohen v. Beneficial Industrial Loan Corp.* 337 U.S. 541, 548 (1949); "[A]bsent the medium of the derivative action, the concept of fiduciary duty might . . . have acquired considerably less substantive meaning." ALI, 225 (T.D. No. 1, 1982).

[2] A formally distinct yet substantively similar classification of the sources of liability is set out in Harvey, *The Public-Spirited Defendant and Others: Liability of Directors and Officers of Not-For-Profit Corporations*, 17 Mar. L. Rev. 665, 675 (1984).

[3] *Id.*, at 700 ("the greatest number of complaints asking relief against officers and directors as individuals allege conflict of interest or wrongful taking of a corporate opportunity").

[4] In some jurisdictions, even members may be denied the right to bring suit unless they possess some interest distinct from that of the general public. *See, e.g., Lopez v. Medford Community Centre, Inc.*, 384 Mass. 163, 424 N.E.2d 229 (1981); *McDaniel v. Frisco Employees Hospital Association*, 510 S.W.2d 752 (Mo. 1974).

[5] Note, *The Nonprofit Corp. in North Carolina: Recognizing a Right to Member Derivative Suits*, 63 N.C. L. Rev. 999, 999 (1985); *see also*, Harvey, *supra*, note 2 at 689-99. The general rule is that one who is merely a possible beneficiary of a charity or a member of a class of possible beneficiaries is not entitled to sue. Instead, the attorney general has the statutory power and duty to represent beneficiaries (although there are some recognized exceptions). The policy reasons are that the limitations on standing prevent vexatious litigation and suits by irresponsible parties who do not have a tangible stake in a matter. This is the traditional view, which has been embodied in most nonprofit corporate laws. There has been little effort to go behind these shibboleths to examine whether the fears of an inundation of litigation is a likely outcome of relaxed standing

rules. By way of contrast, it is interesting to note the differences in according standing to plaintiffs in the business corporation context. The reality is that standing requirements for corporate shareholders are not difficult to comply with. The requisite economic interest is typically a single share of stock and, therefore, the entry barrier is minimal, at least for the publicly traded corporation. Consequently, there are hundreds of derivative suits each year (although they are skewed towards large publicly held corporations). *See generally*, ALI, 229-30, (T.D.No. 4, 1985). The potential class of plaintiffs is enormous as the price of admission to a judicial forum is all but nominal. Without going that far, there might well be an appropriate middle ground between permissive corporate requirements and overly restrictive nonprofit requirements (whether through a requirement of financial support or receipt of services or other tangible nexus by a potential plaintiff to a nonprofit defendant).

[6] *Valle v. North Jersey Automobile Club*, 125 N.J. Super. 302, 310 A.2d 518, 525-26 (1973).

[7] *See also*, Fremont-Smith, *Foundations and Government* 234-241 (1985); Karst, *The Efficiency of the Charitable Dollar; An Unfulfilled State Responsibility*, 73 H. L. Rev. 433, 449-460 (1960).

[8] The National Association of Attorneys General, Committee on the Office of Attorney General, *State Regulation of Charitable Trusts and Solicitations* 8-9, (1977). This tends to support the refrain of supporters of more vigorous enforcement efforts that attorneys general's offices are woefully inadequate to the task they face. *See* Karst, *supra* note 7, at 451-60. *See generally*, Harvey, *supra* note 2.

[9] National Assoc. of Attorneys General, *Consumer Protection Report*, Cumulative Index, Jan.-Dec. 1985. Even where, as in New York, there is a relatively large staff and a tradition of vigilance, the reach of the office is limited and the circumscribed standing rules preclude any substantial number of actions that could lead to the imposition of liability for directors. By way of contrast, the Internal Revenue Service, which has far less extensive authority, has considerably greater resources at its disposal for performing comparable oversight and enforcement functions.

[10] *Stern v. Lucy Webb Hayes National Training School*, 367 F. Supp. 536, (D.D.C 1973), *opinion supplemented by* 381 F.Supp. 1003 (D.D.C. 1974).

[11] *Zehner v. Alexander*, No. 56,1979, slip op. (Comm. Plea, 39th. Dist. Pa. 1979).

[12] *Compare Miller v. Aldherhold*, 228 Ga. 65, 184, S.E.2d 172 (1971), *with Jones v. Grant*, 344 So.2d 1210 (Ala. 1977). *Miller*, a virtually identical case decided just across the border from the seemingly expansive *Jones v. Grant*, without much analysis, simply observes that students have contract rights only and, finding no trust, gives short shrift to the standing argument. *See also, Alco Gravure v. Knapp Foundation*, 64 N.Y.2d 458, 479 N.E.2d 752, 490 N.Y.S.2d 116 (1985) (beneficiary-members of a nonprofit organization had standing to prevent application of funds to any other charitable organization); *Voelker v. St. Louis Mercantile Library*, 359 S.W.2d 689 (Mo. 962) (library members lacked standing to challenge a lease of charitable property).

A number of relatively recent pronouncements, by both state and federal courts, continue to make only the most circumscribed exceptions to the exclusivity of the attorney general's standing to challenge director misconduct. Even the occasionally frank recognition of the pronounced limits on the attorney general's resources does not seem to have moved courts very far toward a liberal standing doctrine. *See City of Paterson v. Paterson General Hospital*, 97 N.J. Super, 514, 235 A.2d 487 (1967) (parties specially interested may sue to compel performance of the purposes of a charitable corporation). Id. at 495. In *Newman v. Forward Lands*, 430 F.Supp. 1320, 1324 (E.D.Pa. 1977), the court determined, in applying Pennsylvania law, that while only the attorney general or a co-trustee may sue generally, a nonprofit with a contractual interest in land allegedly diverted by another nonprofit organization's executive director possessed the requisite "special interest." In *American Center for Education v. Cavnar*, 80 Cal. App. 3d 476, 145 Cal. Rptr. 736 (1978), a former officer was barred on standing grounds from challenging, in the name of the corporation, actions by his former colleagues, notwithstanding the seeming relaxation of standing requirements in *Holt v. College of Osteopathic Physicians and Surgeons*, 394 P.2d 932, 40 Cal. Rptr. 244, (1963); *see also, Veteran's*

Industries, Inc. of Long Beach, Cal. v. Lynch, 8 Cal. App. 3d 902 88 Cal. Rptr. 303, (1970) (two charitable corporations had no standing to intervene in the dissolution and distribution of the assets of a third, unrelated charitable organization, where they could not claim that they fulfilled all the charitable purposes of the dissolving nonprofit); *San Diego County Council, Boy Scouts of America, v. City of Escondido*, 14 Cal. App.3d 189, 92 Cal. Rptr. 186, (1971) (scouting organization specifically intended to benefit from gift of property could challenge a proposed change in property's use). In *Lopez v. Medford*, 384 Mass. 163, 424 N.E.2d 229 (1981), the exclusivity of the attorney general's oversight function is reaffirmed although the court recognized that other grounds for standing may exist if the plaintiff's interests are distinct from those of the general public (already represented by the attorney general). Consequently, members could raise certain claims relating strictly to their membership rights. *See also, Jessie v. Boynton*, 372 Mass. 293, 361 N.E.2d 1267 (1977) (plaintiff hospital employees, who were members of a nonprofit hospital corporation, were allowed to bring a suit to block a vote by other members of the organization that would have changed their status to nonvoting members). Finally, in challenging the administration of health insurance plans by nonprofit health insurance providers, subscribers were denied standing because, among other things, the nonprofit insurance plan's directors owed no duty to plaintiffs-subscribers, but only to the organization they served, *Christiansen v. National Savings and Trust Co.*, 683 F.2d 520 (D.C. Cir. 1982). In reaching this holding, the court sharply limited the scope of the *Sibley Hospital (Stern*, 367 F. Supp. 536) case. The court favorably comments on the lower court's description of *Sibley* as "novel precedent" (*Christiansen*, 683 F.2d at 527) and concluded that Judge Gesell did not create duties of the trustees to the patients, but, in the unique circumstances of that case, merely let the patients enforce a duty of the trustees to the hospital because "there was no one else" to do so (*Id.* at 528).

[13] Ellman, *Driven from the Tribunal: Judicial Resolution of Internal Church Disputes*, 69 Cal. L. Rev. 1378; Hansmann, *Reforming Nonprofit Corporation Law*, 129 U. of Pa. L. Rev. 497, 606–15 (1981); Fishman, *The Development of Nonprofit Corporation Law and an Agenda for Reform*, 34 Emory L.J., 617, 653–56 (1985).

¹⁴ Perhaps broader recognition or use of the "common fund" exception could alter this pattern. The common law allows for the recovery of attorney's fees when members of a class have benefitted through the lawyer's efforts, though he does not directly represent the entire class; otherwise, the nonrepresented members would be enriched unjustly, *Washington Federal Savings & Loan Ass'n v. Village Mall*, 394 N.Y.S.2d 772 (Sup. Ct. Queens Co. 1977). *See also, Sprague v. Taconic Nat. Bank*, 307 U.S. 161, 167, 59 S. Ct. 777, 780 (1939), notwithstanding the uncertainty of their identity, *Boeing Co. v. Van Gemart*, 444 U.S. 472 (1980).

¹⁵ *U.S. v. Mt. Vernon Mortgage Corp.*, 128 F. Supp. 629 (D.D.C. 1954), *aff'd*, 236 F.2d 724 (D.C. Cir. 1956), *cert. denied*, 332 U.S. 988 (1957).

¹⁶ *Mile-O-Mo Fishing Club, Inc. v. Noble*, 62 Ill.App.2d 50, 210 N.E.2d 12 (1965).

¹⁷ *Lynch v. Redfield*, 9 C.A.3d 293, 88 Cal. Rptr. 86 (1970). Even in *Blankenship v. Boyle*, 329 F. Supp. 1089 (D.D.C. 1971) involving UMW pension funds and the now notorious Tony Boyle, Judge Gesell, in seemingly typical fashion, both giveth and taketh away, by initially holding negligent trustees liable for lost income on millions of dollars of unproductive noninterest-bearing accounts and then invoking a short limitations period thereby curtailing their exposure to any judgment. *Id.* at 1112.

¹⁸ *Valle*, 125 N.J.Super. 302, 310 A.2d 518 (1973); *aff'd, as modified*, 141 N.J.Sup. 568, 359 A.2d 504 (1976); *aff'd. as modified*, 74 N.J. 109, 376 A.2D 1192 (1977).

¹⁹ *Mountain Top Youth Camp v. Lyon*, 20 N.C. App. 694, 202 S.E.2d 498 (1974).

²⁰ *People v. Larkin*, 413 F. Supp. 978 (N.D. Cal. 1976). In light of the consistently generous holdings concerning directors' conduct, the rare case in which breaching directors appear to suffer genuine sanctions seems truly abberational (e.g. in *Bolton v. Stillwagon*, 410 Pa. 618, 190 A.2d 105 [1963]). Directors who diverted a corporate opportunity to their personal benefit not only had to reconvey the

diverted property but were unable to recoup the cost of substantial improvements they had made on the property).

[21] *Harrison v. Attorney General*, 31 Conn. Supp. 93, 324 A.2d 279, at 287 (1974). This perhaps understandable reluctance to hold directors financially responsible in the light of their volunteer service is also sometimes seen in a more pernicious form in which a donor's benefactions immunize him from any subsequent lapses or misjudgments. In *George Pepperdine Foundation v. Pepperdine*, 271 P.2d 600 (D.C., C.A. 1954), the founder was exonerated of responsibility for the most egregious losses incurred by the foundation, admittedly caused by misjudgments rather than venal or corrupt behavior, not by having met the requisite standard of care or after a considered analysis of the business judgment rule's safe harbor, but simply by virtue of his having founded and endowed the organization. While perhaps no longer good law in California, (*Holt*, 394 P.2d 932, 40 Cal. Rptr. 244, [1964]), *Pepperdine* is by no means a unique case. A similar attitude is manifest in *Miami Retreat Foundation v. Ervin*, 62 So.2d 748 (Fla. 1952), which, in reversing a lower court's reorganization of the board, observed that "the sole founder . . . should certainly be accorded considerable latitude in . . . administration." *Id.* at 752. The attitude it reflects is more pervasive than one would expect from the few cases that seem to proclaim it explicitly. It is another way in which the applicable legal standards and the realities of nonprofit governance are at odds. What courts most often do with these situations is to dissemble but obscure the bases of decision making. *Pepperdine* and *Miami Retreat* make clear what is often present but unarticulated, *i.e.*, that the law may tolerate excesses by a founder because, in some sense, the founder is regarded in as having a proprietary interest. *See also, Haines v. Elliot*, 58 A. 718 (Conn. 1904).

[22] Report of the Governor's Advisory Commission on Liability Insurance (Jones Commission), *Insuring Our Future* 163 (April 7, 1986).

[23] The survey was conducted in 1984 among the twenty-seven members of the Committee on Non-Profit Organizations of the Association of the Bar of the City of New York. Among other things, the survey called for responses regarding the frequency of claims against nonprofit clients based on issues of fiduciary management

and other potential sources of liability, the size of the claims, and their resolution. Questionnaire from Daniel L. Kurtz, Esq., to Members of the Committee on Philanthropic Associations, Aug. 26, 1985. No claims were reported.

[24] *Francis T. v. Village Green Owners Association*, 229 Cal. Rptr. 456, 463–67 (Cal. 1986); Wolff, *Selecting and Organizing the Not-for-Profit Entity*, in The New York Not-for-Profit Organization 3, 7 (1965); Treusch & Sugarman, *Tax Exempt Charitable Organizations* 29 (1983); The Council of New York Law Associates, *The Legal and Regulatory Affairs Manual* I–1 (1982).

[25] *Merriman v. Smith*, 599 S.W.2d 548 (Tenn. 1979).

[26] ALI, §4.01, Comment (e) (T.D. No. 4, 1985).

[27] *See, e.g., Newman v. Forward Lands*, 430 F.Supp. 1320, 1322 (E.D. Pa. 1977), in which the plaintiff nonprofit organization's claim that the defendant directors had violated duties of loyalty and care were rejected because such duties were strictly duties to their own corporations, not to a third party like the plaintiff corporation. The *Newman* court also rejected an effort to pierce the corporate veil on the grounds that the defendants' conduct was fraudulent, resisting the plaintiff's attempt to equate with fraud negligent or even reckless performance by directors of their duties. In some circumstances, not applicable to nonprofits, officers and directors may have a duty to deal fairly with shareholders. ALI, Intro. Note, Part V, Comment (b) (T.D. No. 4, 1985).

[28] *Stern*, 367 F. Supp. 536 (D.D.C 1973) *opinion supplemented by* 381 F.Supp. 1003 (D.D.C. 1974). The *Sibley* court, in an earlier opinion rejected a class action that would have permitted third party recovery.

[29] Many states make such provision by statute. See e.g., Montana Nonprofit Corporation Act §35–2–411.

[30] *Godwin-Bevers, Co. v. V.G.P. Enterprises, Inc.*, 502 P.2d 1124 (Colo. App. 1972).

[31] *Dupack v. Nationwide Leisure Corp.* 70 A.D.2d 568, 417 N.Y.S.2d 63 (1979) (individual officer can be liable for fraudulent misrepresentation in connection with a contract, although not for breach of contract itself). 417 N.Y.S.2d at 65.

[32] Although the corporate veil is typically pierced to reach an owner and, strictly speaking, nonprofits have no owner, the doctrine still has applicability to nonprofits. In *Macaluso v. Jenkins*, 95 Ill. App. 3d 461, 50 Ill. Dec. 934, 420 N.E.2d 251 (1981), the chief executive officer of a nonprofit organization was personally liable for an unpaid printing bill of the organization because the corporation had no genuine separate existence. It was merely the officer's *alter ego.* It is noteworthy, however, that in rejecting the liability for another officer, the court concluded that nonprofits were under no obligation to have adequate capital and that anyone dealing with a nonprofit presumably was on notice that the nonprofit had limited resources. The court also flatly rejected the notion that as an officer, the employee violated a fiduciary duty to creditors, concluding that, generally, no such duty to creditors exists and that creditors deal at arm's-length. The situation would be different, however, if the officer had fraudulently induced the party to enter into the printing contract. *But c.f., Lake Otis Clinic, Inc. v. State*, 650 P.2d 388 (Alaska 1982).

[33] H.G. Henn & J.R. Alexander, *Laws of Corporations*, 582, 607 (1983); *Burke v. Musarra*, 46 Misc.2d 933, 261 N.Y.S.2d 314 (Sup. Ct. N.Y. Co. 1965) (the court would not dismiss a case seeking damages from a corporate officer who signed, as a corporate officer, a criminal information leading to the arrest of the plaintiff for vandalism, a charge subsequently dismissed); *La Lumea v. Schwartz*, 23 A.D.2d 668, 257 N.Y.S.2d 348, 9 A.D. 2 (1965) (corporate officer participating in invasion of privacy tort may be held responsible); *Lahr v. Adell Chemical Co.*, 300 F.2d 256 (1st Cir. 1962) (action for defamation may lie against corporate officer "whether or not he was acting within the scope of his authority."). *Id.* at 260; *Francis T. Green* 229 Cal. Rptr. 456 (condominium association board members liable to plaintiff unit owner for injuries caused by third party due to inadequate security system). *See also, Seligson v. N.Y. Produce Exchange*, 378 F. Supp. 1076 (S.D.N.Y.

1974) ("a director's common law liability for his tort persists [even] . . . within the scope of his corporate duties") *Id.* at 1092.

[34] "The substantive law may make liability difficult to establish." *Jones Commission Report, supra* 34 note 22 at 162.

[35] In *Zubik v. Zubik,* 384 F.2d 267 (3d Cir. 1967), the court noted, in considering an effort to impose individual liability on a corporate principal, that "counsel has been unable to cite a case where the corporate entity was disregarded to make an individual liable for tort." *Id.* at 273, n. 14. This, of course, contrasts with liability for contracts and other obligations in cases where piercing the corporation veil is appropriate. *See, supra,* cases cited in note 32. In response to the current insurance crises, states have had a variety of responses to the tort liability problem. New York has imposed a "gross negligence" standard to establish director liability in the ordinary tort case. N.Y. Not-for-Profit Corp. Law, §720-a (1987 Supplement) N.Y. Civ. Prac. Law §3211 (1987 Supplement) adopted at the same time, creates a procedure to dispose summarily of spurious third party tort claims.

[36] For example, the conduct of illegal gambling activities by a non-profit social club may result in individual liability. *Veterans Service Club v. Sweeney,* 252 S.W. 2d 25 (Ky. 1952); *Beale v. Kappa Alpha Order,* 192 Va. 382, 64 S.E.2d 789, 798 (1951). Some states have codified this legal doctrine. *See, e.g.,* N.Y. Penal Law §320.25 (McKinney's 1970).

[37] Note *Corporations: Illegal Activities by Non-Profit Corporations,* 8 Ark. L. Rev. 110 (1953–54).

[38] *See, e.g.,* Ill. Gen. Not-for Profit Corporation Act §66; Indiana Not-for Profit Corp. Act §64; and, *inter alia,* statutes cited in Harvey, *supra* note 2 at 732 n. 348–91.

[39] Rev. Ruling 84–83, I.R.B. 1984–24, 13; *Hildebrand Jr. v. U.S.,* 563 F. Supp. 1255 (D.N.J. 1983); *but c.f., Schwinger v. U.S.,* 652F. Supp. 464 (E.D.N.Y. 198) and *Simpson v. U.S.,* 664 F. Supp. 43 (E.D.N.Y. 1987). *See also,* Conn. G.S. §12–449; IRC §4941, Reg.

§53.4941(a)–(1)(b) and 53.4941(b)–1(b); IRC §4945, Reg. §53.4945–1(a)(2) and 53.4945–1(c).

[40] *United States v. Park*, 421 U.S. 658 (1975) (corporate president convicted of Food Drug & Cosmetic Act violations, as a "responsible" corporate official regardless of awareness of wrongdoing). The analogy to nonprofits is imperfect because for-profit corporate officers are typically employees, while nonprofit officers generally are not. This make imposition of this type of liability in the nonprofit context even less likely.

[41] *See, e.g., Hot Seats, Board Members Draw Fire, and Some Think Twice About Serving*, Wall Street J., Feb. 5, 1986, at 1, col. 1.

[42] *See supra*, note 22 at 163.

[43] Delaware has a single statute that applies to business and nonprofit corporations. Organizations formed in that state may benefit from recent changes in its laws expanding indemnification and contracting the scope of liability. How they apply to nonprofits, however, remains uncertain (*e.g.*, some states, such as New York, will continue to apply their own law on liability to New-York-based organizations, even if formed elsewhere).

[44] *See supra*, note 22, at 163.

[45] Ohio Revised Code §2305.38 (effective Oct. 14, 1986).

[46] Illinois Not For Profit Corp. Act §24b.

[47] Tenn. Gen. Corp. Act 48–1–852.

[48] Some of the "tort reform" states may be subject to challenge on grounds similar to the attacks on tort reform measures intended to alleviate the medical malpractice insurance crisis. *See, e.g. Arneson v. Olson*, 270 N.W.2d 125 (N.D. 1978).

[49] New York complemented its tort reform measures (Not-for-Profit Corp. Law 720–a imposing a "gross negligence" standard for lia-

bility) by adding a provision to its civil procedure law enabling defending directors to obtain a prompt and early dismissal of any action where there is not a "reasonable probability" of gross negligence. C.P.L.R. §3211 (1987 Supplement). Unfortunately, most other states adopting tort reform procedures have no such "procedural sidekick" and, perhaps, remain vulnerable to more artful pleading.

[50] State of N.Y. Dept. of Insurance, *Circular Letter No. 15* (Sept. 10, 1986).

Chapter Six

[1] For example, a number of commentaries on governance express directly contrasting views of the scope of common law indemnification doctrine. Klink, Chalif, Bishop, Jr. and Arsht, *Liabilities which Can Be Covered under State Statutes and Corporate By-Laws*, 27 Bus. Law. 109 (1971); *but c.f.*, Moody, *State Statutes Governing Directors of Charitable Corporations*, 18 Univ. of .S.F. L. Rev. 749, 774 (1984).

[2] It is striking that much of the discussion of D&O policies at a 1971 ABA National Institute remains substantially current. Hinsey, Delancey, Stahl and Kramer, *What Existing D&O Policies Cover*, 27 Bus. Law. 147 (1971). More recently, a 1978 article by Joseph F. Johnston, Jr., *Corporate Indemnification and Liability Insurance for Directors*, 33 Bus. Law. 1993 (1978), is still regarded as authoritative.

[3] *Kanneberg v. Evangelical Creed Congregation*, 131 N.W. 353 (Wis. 1911); *Cross v. Midtown Club, Inc.*, 33 Conn. Supp. 150, 365, A.2d 1227 (Super. Ct. 1976); *Texas Society v. Fort Bend Chapter*, 590 S.W.2d 156 (Tex. Civ. App. 1979); *Thisted v. Tower Management Corporation*, 409 P.2d 813 (Mont. 1966).

[4] Contrast, for example, the court's tortured reasoning in *New York Dock Company, Inc. v. McCollum*, 173 Misc. 106, 16 N.Y.S.2d 844 (Sup. Ct. Onondega Co. 1939), with *Kanneberg*, 131 N.W. 353

(Wis. 1911). The policy favoring broad indemnification is well articulated in *Kanneberg*:

> Whenever the right of a corporation or its . . . representatives to do a particular thing . . . is challenged . . . such . . . officers have the moral and legal right to stand by their judgment in the matter, and it is their duty to the corporation to do so . . . and if that brings . . . an efficient . . . challenge to defend in court . . . it is their duty to respond to the attack. . . .
>
> The right to defend . . . included . . . the right to employ . . . attorneys . . . The right to employ counsel necessarily carried with it the duty to pay counsel . . . regardless of the outcome. Such right . . . did not depend upon who was right in the controversy."

Id. at 355.

The gist of the countervailing policy, as expressed in *New York Dock*, seems strained, at odds with common sense: that the corporation, being an actual defendant itself, gained nothing from the directors' vindication it would not have gained from its own defense and, therefore, it received no benefit. *Id.* at 848–49.

[5] Klink, Chalif, Bishop, Jr. and Arsht, *supra*, note 1, at 111; Johnston, Jr., *supra*, note 2, at 1995–96; Moody, *supra*, note 1, at 765 n. 76. However, while all states have some indemnification provisions for business corporations, several states still lack any indemnity provision for nonprofits and, in such states, presumably common law principles still would be applicable.

[6] *See, e.g.*, N.Y. Bus. Corp. Law §721–722, Del. Gen. Corp. Law §145 *et. al.*

[7] The underlying policy may even have greater force in the nonprofit context where, typically, service is entirely uncompensated while, increasingly, directors of business corporations are well rewarded for board service in addition to enjoying the indirect, financial benefits that may accrue because of the contextual corporate culture. *See also*, RMNCA, Sub-Chapter E—Indemnification, Introductory Comments (Exposure Draft, 1986).

NOTES

[8] RMBCA §8.44, at 240. Indeed, even with traditional corporate indemnity policies, recruits for corporate boards are harder to attract because of fears of increased exposure and the costs of protection. *News from Korn/Ferry International*, June 3, 1986. According to a survey by the Wyatt Company, Chicago, Ill., per claim cost of defense under a business directors' and officers' liability insurance policy rose from $181,500 in 1974 to $461,000 in 1984. *The New York Times*, March 7, 1986, at 81, col. 2.

[9] Moody, *supra*, note 1, at 764.

[10] The provision is essentially an enabling provision and provides as follows:

> 87. To indemnify any director or officer or former director or officer of the corporation, or any person who may have served at its request as a director or officer of another corporation in which it owns shares of capital stock or of which it is a creditor, against expenses actually and reasonably incurred by him in connection with the defense of any action, suit or proceeding, civil or criminal, in which he is made a party by reason of being or having been such director or officer, except in relation to matters as to which he shall be adjudged in such action, suit or proceeding to be liable for negligence or misconduct in the performance of duty to the corporation; and to make any other indemnification that shall be authorized by the articles of incorporation or by-laws, or resolution adopted after notice by the members entitled to vote."

Model Nonprofit Corp. Act §5(n) (1964).

[11] The RMBCA, while making significant organizational changes, effected no major substantive alteration in this area. Block, Barton and Radin, *Indemnification and Insurance of Corporate Officials: Officers' and Directors' Liability: A Review of the Business Judgment Rule*, Directors & Officers Liability Insurance & Self-Insurance 613 (1986).

[12] A clear majority of states have indemnification provisions for non-profits derived from the MBCA or modeled after a state's business corporation law provisions. Brown, *The Not-for-Profit Corporate*

Director: Legal Liabilities and Protection, 28 Fed'n of Ins. Couns. Q. 57 (1977–78). However, unlike the duties of obedience, care, and loyalty, which remain primarily products of the common law, indemnification today is virtually an exclusively statutory creature. Because this chapter is not an all-state survey, it is impossible, within the limited confines of this book, to discuss every important statutory difference. Readers are especially cautioned, therefore, to be aware that any general discussion must be qualified by a careful review of the law of a particular state.

[13] The old Model Act does permit broader indemnification, but only if authorized in the charter or by-laws, or for those relatively few organizations with members, by a resolution approved by members after proper notice. Both unlikely eventualities for most nonprofits.

[14] No statute is exclusive with respect to agents and employees and some afford officers broader latitude than directors. Block, Barton & Radin, *supra*, note 11, at 621; Olsen, Bogen & McGill, *Non-Insurance Alternatives for Directors and Officer Protection*, in The Crisis in Directors and Officers Liability Insurance 313 (Law & Bus., HBJ 1986); *See generally, Memo to Corporate Clients of Bryan, Cave, McPheeters and McRoberts Re: Directors & Officers Liability Insurance & Indemnification Agreements*, XI The Corporate Counsel, Appendix (March–April 1986).

[15] Del. Gen. Corp. Law §145(f).

[16] *See, e.g.* 42 Pa. Cons. Stat. §8361 *et seq* (1986 Supplementary Pamphlet).

[17] Some jurisdictions, notably Delaware, permit partial indemnification when there is partial success. Del. Gen. Corp. Law §145(c) ("[t]o the extent that [the person to be indemnified] has been successful . . . he shall be indemnified"). See *US v. Wolfson*, 437 F.2d 862 (2nd Cir. 1970); Barton, *Indemnification of Corp. Officials*, Strategies for Responding to the D&O Insurance Crises 21(Law & Bus., Prentice-Hall 1986).

[18] Not all however. Those 10 states still following the old MNCA make no such distinction.

[19] This would be so whether or not, as in New York, the attorney general may also exercise rights of members or a director. Such actions are clearly derivative in nature. N.Y. Not-for-Profit Corp. Law, §706(d), §720(b).

[20] It is important to note that a determination in a consent decree may not lead to the same result, thus permitting indemnification. *Cambridge Fund, Inc. v. Abells*, 501 F. Supp. 598, 617 (S.D.N.Y. 1980).

[21] N.Y. Bus. Corp. Law §722; 15 Pa. Cons. Stat. §7742.

[22] RMNCA 8.51(a)(3); N.Y. Not-for-Profit Corp. Law 723(a); Del. Gen. Corp. Law §145(a).

[23] Of particular importance in this period of nonprofit entrepreneurship is the coverage most, although not all, statutes give directors who serve at the indemnifying corporation's request on another board (*e.g.*, that of a for-profit subsidiary, a related nonprofit or joint venture). Del. Gen. Corp. Law §145; N.Y. Not-for-Profit Corp. Law §723(a); RMNCA §8.50(2).

[24] Ca. Gen. Corp. Law §317(b).

[25] Presumably independent or special legal counsel means a lawyer or firm that does not regularly or generally represent the organization and has no other significant ties to the organization or its directors. Ohio, alone among the states, defines this by limiting independence to lawyers who have not performed legal services for the corporation for at least five years. Ohio Non-Profit Gen. Corp. Law §1702.12(E)(4).

[26] In at least one state, Texas, it is clear that the statutory omission precludes the advancement of costs. In *Texas Society v. Fort Bend Chapter*, 590 S.W.2d 156 (Tex. Civ. App. 1979), the court held that the use of charitable funds in advance of judgment when not specifically authorized by statute was *ultra vires*, i.e., beyond the power of the corporation to do. *See also*, similar result in *Thisted v. Tower Management Corporation* 409 P.2d 813 (Mont. 1966) (Montana had no statutory indemnification provision).

[27] In states with indemnification provisions based on the Model Acts, the finding that a director has met the requisite standard of conduct to qualify for an advance of defense costs may be based on the facts "then known," reflecting the inherent difficulty of making the requisite finding at precisely that early stage of a litigation when an advance of defense costs is most needed. Delaware recently eliminated the necessity for individual determinations of a director's application for advancement of expenses. See Del. Gen. Corp. Law §145(e) (amended July 1, 1986).

[28] Del. Gen. Corp. Law §145 (e); 42 Pa. Cons. Stat. §8365(d) (1986 Supplementary Pamphlet).

[29] Johnston, *supra*, note 2, at 2010. *See also*, Sparks, Johnston & Conan, *Indemnification and Directors' and Officers' Liability: The Legal Framework under Delaware Law*, in The Crisis in Directors' and Officers' Liability Insurance 3, 19–22 (1986); *Memo to Corporate Clients of Bryan, Cave, McPheeters and McRoberts Re: Directors & Officers Liability Insurance & Indemnification Agreements*, XI The Corporate Counsel, Appendix (March–April 1986).

[30] Insurers use a variety of names for these policies: Directors' and Officers' Legal Liability, Executive Liability, etc.

[31] Special concerns remain for foundations that purchase D&O policies. The premium payments, when added to other compensation received by the directors, must be "reasonable" if the purchase of insurance is not to be considered a violation of the prohibition on self-dealing. Treas. Reg. §53.4941(d)–2(f)(1).

[32] Some insurers issue a single policy form with two separate insuring clauses, but most insurers still active in the market issue a single policy in two parts, which makes for confusing reading. *See* Conley & Vitlin, *Form & Structure of the Directors' and Officers Policy: Conditions & Cancellation Provisions* in D&O Liability 161, 161–62 (PLI 1986).

[33] *See* Goldwasser, *Scope and Coverage of Directors' and Officers' Liability Policies*, in D&O Liability 173, 191–93 (PLI 1986).

[34] The reverse situation—a business corporation officer or director sitting on a nonprofit board—typically would be covered by his employee's D&O policy where such service is at its request. This is a common situation for any large complex business enterprise.

[35] The insuring clause's "pay on behalf of" would seem to require defense costs be advanced when such costs are included within the definition of loss, as the defense costs or loss is necessarily incurred during the pendency of the litigation. *See* Lazar, *Form & Structure of Defense & Settlement Clauses in D&O Policies*, in D&O Liability 235, 270–73 (1986 PLI).

[36] Nevertheless the list should be reasonably exhaustive. Nonprofits have the luxury, denied to many publicly held businesses, of not fearing premature or incomplete disclosures of potential liabilities that might affect the market for its securities, nor do they have an SEC to worry about in making such disclosures.

[37] These can often be covered by other fiduciary policies.

[38] *Bird v. Penn Central*, 334 F. Supp. 255 (E.D. Pa. 1971), *on rehearing*, 341 F. Supp. 291 (E.D. Pa. 1972); *Shapiro v. American Home Assurance Co.*, 584 F. Supp. 1245 (D. Mass. 1984).

[39] When compared to premiums for general liability policies and the rate of increase in such premiums, the cost of D&O policies may still appear to be modest.

[40] State of N.Y., Dept. of Insurance, *Circular Letter No. 15* (Sept. 10, 1986).

INDEX

INDEX

INDEX

INDEX

standards of, 23–24, 61, 64, 95

Ultra vires activities, 89
Uniform Management of
    Institutional Funds Act, 12

Volunteers
  as board members, 18, 94, 99,
    113
  as officers, 19

recruitment of, 17

Wilson college case, and standing
    to sue, 93
Withholding taxes, 86
Wrongful acts. *See also* Criminal
    actions
  and D&O insurance, 111–113
  and indemnification, 105
  standing to sue in, 93